BEAN CUISINE

BEAN CUISINE

A Culinary Guide for the
ECOGOURMET

BY BEVERLY WHITE
ILLUSTRATED BY JULIE MAAS

Routledge & Kegan Paul
London and New York

First published in Great Britain in 1977
by Routledge & Kegan Paul Ltd
11 New Fetter Lane, London EC4P 4EE
Published in the USA by
Routledge & Kegan Paul Inc.
in association with Methuen Inc.
29 West 35th Street, New York NY 10001
Reprinted in 1978, 1980, 1984 and 1987
Printed in Great Britain by
T. J. Press (Padstow) Ltd
Padstow, Cornwall

British Library Cataloguing in Publication Data

White, Beverly

Bean cuisine.
1. Cookery (Beans)
I. Title
641.6'5'65 TX803.B4   76.77487

ISBN 0-7100-8759-4

To Jane Hodges, Mila Sorensen, David White, Tom Fiero, and the Emma Steffens Commune for all their tasty advice.

CONTENTS

3   BEAN SALADS   37

4   BEAN SANDWICHES, SPREADS, AND SUCH   49

5   STOVETOP BEANPOTS   61

6   OVEN BEANPOTS   89

INTRODUCTION

"The world is so full of a number of beans, I'm sure we should all eat happy as Queens."

Bean cuisine is relatively unknown. Even the art of baking beans in the traditional manner has been all but lost. There is pea soup, of course, navy bean and lentil soups, and three-bean salad, but that's about all. Few cooks, gourmet or otherwise, know how to cook black beans, pinto beans, soybeans, or garbanzos, to mention only a few of the many dry varieties available in both supermarkets, continental and health food shops across the country.*

But the cooks in our culture today who want to learn the art of legume cookery are growing in numbers. Those who are ecologically concerned are interested in bean dishes that are not dependent upon the addition of meat for their savour. They are the informed people of our times who know that meat—particularly the fat in meat—can be a powerful factor in the creation of potentially harmful cholesterol in the human blood stream. And they know that meat is being blamed increasingly by scientists as a contributing factor to the high incidence of colonic cancer in Western countries.

These cooks also know what nutritional scientists have come to know only in recent years: that vegetable protein—if various sources of it are included in one meal—can provide for tissue growth and regeneration. The few protein components lacking in many legumes are contained more abundantly in grains and nuts; while those lacking in grains and nuts are usually present

*See the **International Vegetarian Health Food Handbook,** ed: Joanna Lawton (The Vegetarian Society of the UK Ltd 1977) for a detailed shopping guide.

in legumes. Furthermore, eating beans and grains at the same meal makes *all* of the essential amino acids present in these foods assimilable, since they must all be present simultaneously for the body to absorb them. And, as a result, up to 43 percent more protein is derived from these foods in combination than if they are eaten at different times.* (Apart from their virtues as sources of proteins, beans can be commended for their other nutritional values as well. In general, they are high in iron, potassium, calcium, vitamin A, thiamine, and vitamin C.)

The enlightened cook is also aware of the necessity of living low on the food chain (as well as the potential of living high on the bean!). As human population growth exerts more and more pressure upon the resources of the earth, we must learn to be less dependent upon animals as intermediaries in providing us with the protein substances we need—and which the earth provides so abundantly in plant life. (The plant life in legumi-nous plants also returns life-giving nitrogen to the soil!) To illustrate: Harvest the soybeans from one acre of land. Feed them to an animal. Slaughter the animal. If you then provide one human being with the meat from that animal, he will have enough protein food for 77 days. The same amount of soy-beans consumed directly by a human being will provide him with protein food for 6.1 years!

To know how we human beings exploit the earth (and the animal life thereon) is one thing. To assimilate this knowledge is another. And to find adequate and satisfying ways of adapting to this new understanding of ourselves in relation to the earth requires ingenuity.

I am confident that one response to our earth's crisis will be the emergence in our culture of a new breed: the bean cook,

---

*See **Diet for a Small Planet** by Frances Moore Lappé (New York: Ballantine Books, Inc., 1971) for a well-documented discussion of this subject.

highly skilled in the art of preparing beans in combination with grains, nuts, and vegetables to complete their protein value. The most skilful of these cooks will also know how to prepare bean dishes of gourmet quality from relatively inexpensive and readily available ingredients, and in this manner make the art accessible to rich and poor alike. The most liberated of these cooks will be men and women who associate gourmet fare with a simple, uncluttered existence, and with one- and two-dish meals that require a minimum of kitchen drudgery *and* a minimum of fuel to prepare.

The message here is clear and plain: "The Bean and Its Friends Are the Way." The compiler is grateful to all those cooks of the past and present who have discovered the tastiness of bean cuisine and have shared their savoury dishes and their recipes with others. When large numbers of cooks jump on the bean wagon, there will be the promise of bean cookery's becoming a highly perfected culinary art. With this hoped for development, the excessive dependence on animal food will decline; and, as a result, there will be more space for the cultivation of legumes and other vegetable proteins, less exploitation of the earth's fish and animal life, and more food for the hungry human beings throughout this world.

GUIDE TO AMERICAN MEASURES

Warning: Red (Azuki) beans are poisonous unless boiled rapidly
for 10 minutes during the cooking process.

Fluid measures

USA	UK
1 US quart	32 fluid oz
1 US pint	16 fluid oz
1 US cup	8 fluid oz
1 US tablespoon	½ fluid oz
3 US teaspoons	½ fluid oz

Dry measures

US cup	
butter	8 oz
fresh breadcrumbs	1 oz
flour	4 oz
milk, light cream	9 oz
rice	6½ oz
seedless raisins	6 oz
sugar	4½ oz
syrup and honey	11½ oz

1 BECOMING A BEAN COOK

"A good bean is not hard to find."

This book, an introduction to the art of the bean, draws upon the bean cuisine that has existed for centuries in many countries around the world, as well as upon recipes that are now being developed and shared by the ecogeneration in this country. It focuses on bean entrées—soups, salads, stews, beancakes, curries, casseroles—which should provide the eco-gourmet with ideas for as much versatility in planning meals around the bean as is traditionally possible with meals centred around meat. It also provides menu suggestions with almost every recipe, to assist the cook in providing the necessary balance of protein foods for optimum nutrition, and to free him/her from the meat-potato-vegetable-salad stereotype. Every recipe has the potential for delicious goodness depending upon the amount of love, care, and good taste devoted to its preparation.

Of course, beans don't have to be dressed up in the ways recipes in this book suggest. Just by themselves, cooked to the point of tenderness and enhanced with a little butter and salt, they are a delicious addition to any meal. The recipes I provide are only an extra enticement in the direction of the Bean Way. Once that is found, "A jug of wine, a loaf of bread, a pot of beans, and Thou," should happily be enough!

About the Recipes

"A bean a day keeps the doctor away."

Several kinds of beans, including black-eyed peas, Great Northern beans, garbanzos, butter beans, kidney beans, and soybeans, can be bought already cooked in cans and can provide the busy person a quick way to prepare many of the dishes in this book.

Almost all of the ingredients called for are relatively inexpensive (or call for small quantities of expensive ingredients, such as rum) and are easily accessible. Fresh ginger may be one exception to this. It is available throughout the year at specialty food shops, especially those which sell Oriental and Continental foods, and at large supermarkets at certain times of the year. Several ginger roots can be bought at once and frozen; it keeps best this way and can easily be grated in its frozen state. If fresh ginger is unavailable, the powdered form can be used, although the taste is considerably different.

While domestic curry powder can be found in any grocer's, Indian curry powder is far superior and keeps indefinitely if kept tightly covered.

To make bean dishes really delicious, it is important to use quality oils and shortenings. Refined corn oil, safflower oil, peanut oil, and sesame oil are good choices. Olive oil is most appropriate for Middle Eastern, Greek, French, and Italian dishes. Unsalted margarine has few additives and less saturated fat than butter.

Most of the recipes in this book will serve three to four people with an average serving of 3/4 cup. (One can estimate that one cup of dried beans will yield 2 to 2 1/2 cups of cooked beans.)

Buying and Storing Dried Beans

"What this country needs is a good cheap bean."

Dried beans are readily available in most supermarkets, and

can be bought in bulk. (A pound of dried beans should provide 7 to 9 servings.)

They keep indefinitely, and can be stored conveniently in covered containers. (Whole grains can also be stored in this way.) No electric or human energy is necessary for the preservation of dried beans!

Equipment

"Every bean must have its pot."

It is possible to be a successful bean cook with no more special equipment than an asbestos pad (if one uses a gas stove) to spread the heat gently and evenly under the bean kettle. Cooking beans on the top of the stove, however, requires a great deal of time and considerable attention from the cook; it also requires more fuel. This book assumes that the bean cook will have purchased a *pressure cooker* as standard equipment, though instructions for cooking without pressure are also included here. (See pages 8–9 for a detailed discussion of pressure cookers.)

Another desirable piece of equipment is a *food mill*, available at any hardware or department store. This is invaluable as it can be used both for puréeing and straining bean mixtures.

A *blender* is valuable for grinding seeds and nuts, for blending liquids, and for liquefying and puréeing, although it cannot, like a food mill, remove skins and seeds from a mixture.

A *food grinder* is valuable for grinding beans, nuts, and vegetables.

Bean sprouting devices are available in some health food

stores and some hardware and department stores. Their use eliminates the need for rinsing the sprouts three times a day.

Basic Bean Preparation

"A bean in the pot is worth two on the hoof."

Before soaking any of the dried legumes, it is good to look them over while they are dry to make sure there are not little stones or desiccated kernels present. Packaged beans available in supermarkets usually require little or no examination; this is not always the case, however, with those bought in bulk at wholesalers.

They should then be *well* rinsed before soaking.

To Soak or Not to Soak the Bean . . . and How

Use plenty of water for soaking the bean: about two quarts to one cup of beans. (Be sure to discard the liquid that remains at the end of the soaking period, and add fresh water for cooking; this helps remove the oligosaccharides that cause flatulence.)

The amount of time necessary to soak beans depends on the dryness of the bean, the hardness of the water, and the temperature of the water. If the beans are boiled for 2 to 5 minutes at the beginning of the soaking period, and then allowed to stand for approximately ten hours at room temperature (70°F.), they can be cooked to the point of tenderness and maximum digestibility in the shortest amount of time. One way to test whether the bean has been sufficiently soaked is to break one in two: if the colour is the same at the centre and the outer edge, and if one can easily break each half crosswise into halves, it is ready to be cooked. If, however, tiny bubbles have begun to form on the surface of the water, the bean has been soaked too long (but it can still be used).

Using the above method, beans can be put to soak about the time the morning coffee is brewed and be ready at 5:00 P.M. for the preparation of most of the recipes in this book.

Another method for soaking beans (which requires a little more time and attention on the part of the cook) is to cook the dry beans for 30 minutes, then turn off the heat and let them stand for 1 1/2 to 2 hours before pressure cooking them.

When beans have been in storage for a long time and are very dry, or if the water is very hard, a little baking soda in the soaking water will appreciably shorten the length of time necessary to tenderize them. How much soda to use depends on the hardness of the water. With most tap waters, adding 1/2 teaspoon of soda per quart of water will shorten the cooking time considerably. The soda should be measured *carefully* and added to the soaking water at the start, then poured off when the soaking water is drained. Too much soda will affect the flavour and nutritive value of the bean.

Some legumes require no soaking at all if they are to be cooked under pressure. These include split peas, lentils, and black-eyed peas.

Pressure Cooking

All dried legumes can most conveniently be cooked in a pressure cooker. This method not only saves considerable time, labour, and fuel, but it also ensures the digestibility of these foods. Beans cooked under pressure to the point of real tenderness cause little or no flatulence, and for this reason "bean fare" can be equally acceptable to the young, old, and even the infirm. There may be some individual differences in the ability to digest beans and other legumes—even the most tenderly cooked ones; this being so, the family cook must experiment with various types of legumes to determine which ones are the most digestible as well as the most appetizing. "To each his own bean." And one must allow for the digestive system to accustom itself to the change from a diet largely based on meat (low in fibre content) to one based on vegetables (high in fibre content).

The flatulence problem associated with eating beans is caused by sugars called oligosaccharides, which need to be broken down into digestible form by the soaking and cooking process before they can be properly assimilated by the body. If they are not transformed into simpler sugars during cooking, bacteria attack them when they reach the small intestine, producing intestinal "gas." Therefore, the secret to digestibility of beans is not the addition of baking soda, or meat tenderizer, or turmeric, as some people may say, but thorough soaking and then cooking to the point of tenderness.

Whole grains, which complement legumes in their protein components, also gain in flavour, texture, and digestibility from pressure cooking. This is particularly true of such natural grains as brown rice, oat groats, wild rice, bulgur (pre-cooked cracked wheat), wheat berries, and rye berries, which would otherwise require a long cooking period. (Refined flours and cereals also contain the complementary amino acids, but in smaller amounts.)

Vegetables too—particularly root vegetables—lend themselves favourably to pressure cooking. (Both root and green vegetables contribute amino acids to the diet, but in smaller quantities per average serving than beans.) If they are cooked in water without pressure, the sugar content of the vegetable is bled out into the cooking water, and the flavour and vitamins resident in their volatile oils are driven off in the steam. Under pressure, using as little as one cup of cooking water, both flavour and vitamins are preserved, and the cooking time is considerably reduced: carrots cook in five minutes, potatoes in ten or fifteen.

A pressure cooker is an expensive kitchen implement, but it will last a lifetime or longer. All of its small parts—even those for obsolete models—are available at general supply stores when replacements are needed. Properly and frequently used, it will pay for itself many times. Models in stainless steel, cast, and stamped aluminium are available. The cast aluminium, to my mind, is the best because a) aluminium conducts heat more evenly than steel, and b) food is less likely to stick in a cast-aluminium cooker.

The typical cooker comes in 4-, 6-, and 12-qt sizes (in addition to the large cookers used for canning and institutional cooking). The 6-qt is by far the most economical and convenient to buy, since it can be used successfully with small or large quantities of food. Furthermore, you can fill it as much as half full with no danger of its boiling over the sides.

It is important to know whether the cooker you own cooks at 10-lb pressure or 15-lb pressure. A 15-lb pressure cooker is preferable because foods cooked in it will be done in half the time.

A pressure cooker is simple and safe to use. It usually consists of a pot and its cover, which has a rubber gasket surrounding its inside ring, a vent pipe in the centre, a safety valve (also called an automatic air vent) situated off centre, and a pressure cap or regulator which is placed on the vent pipe during the cooking process. For a cooker of this construction, the directions for use are as follows:

1. Place the material to be cooked in the cooker.* *Fill no more than half full of food and water.* (Remember to use fresh water, not the soaking water.)

2. *Add at least 1 tbsp oil* to prevent the contents from foaming up when they begin to boil, and any seed coats from clogging the steam escape valve.

3. Place the cover on securely.

4. Heat to boiling. Let steam escape for one minute.

5. Place the pressure regulator on the vent pipe.

6. Set the cooker on high heat until the pressure regulator begins to rock gently. Start counting cooking time.

7. Reduce heat to maintain a slow, steady, rocking motion of the pressure regulator.

8. Cook the beans until tender. Recommended times can be only approximate because of such variables as the age of the bean, the amount of soaking time, the hardness of the water, the type of bean, etc. Soybeans, for instance, contain a substance called "trypsin inhibitor" (TI), which obstructs the functioning of a pancreatic enzyme that is essential for the digestion of protein. Thorough cooking of the soybean will inactivate this inhibitor. Nutritionists recommend the following cooking times:

	15-lb pressure	*10-lb pressure*
a) *Hardest Bean*		
Soybean	25–30 min.	50–60 min.
b) *Hard Beans*		
Great Northerns,	10–15 min.	25–30 min.
kidney beans,		
whole peas,		
red beans,		
black beans, garbanzos		
(chickpeas),		
brown beans		

*Any acid substances such as vinegar, tomatoes, fruit juice, or molasses will keep the skins of beans leathery if it is added at the beginning of the cooking period. Therefore, for pressure cooking a dish that includes any of these ingredients it is best to cook—or at least partially cook—the beans before any ingredients of this kind are added.

c) *Soft Beans*
    Lima beans, pink beans,   10 min.   20 min.
    pinto beans, navy beans
d) *Softest Beans*
    Split peas, black-eyed peas,   6–10 min.   15 min.
    lentils (soaking unnecessary)

9. At the end of the cooking period (or at any time before that, in order to check on the contents), totally reduce the interior pressure by setting the whole cooker under a cold tap, or in a pan of cold water. Or let the pressure drop by turning off the heat and letting the cooker stand for 4–5 minutes. There is less likelihood that the skins will break if the pressure is allowed to rise and fall gradually.

10. As soon as no steam escapes when the pressure regulator is tilted, and the plunger in the safety valve has dropped, remove the pressure regulator.

11. Remove the cover.

The cooker of standard construction is equipped with two safety devices: the pressure regulator, which will merely drop off if the pressure gets too high, causing the steam to shoot out in a vertical direction from the vent pipe; and the safety valve, or automatic air vent, which will automatically release excess steam in case the vent pipe becomes clogged so that pressure does not release normally. Therefore there is no real danger of a pressure cooker's exploding.

The manufacturers of pressure cookers provide full instructions for use with the purchase of a new cooker, or at any time in response to a request for instructions, advice, or new parts.

Cooking Beans Without Pressure

1. Use a heavy-bottomed pan, or an asbestos pad under a regular saucepan.

2. Add water or broth to cover the bean mixture generously.

3. Add 1 tbsp oil to each cup of beans to prevent them from foaming up while cooking.

4. Use gentle heat to keep the mixture simmering, never boiling.

5. Stir very little, since frequent stirring causes bean skins to break.

6. Add water if necessary.

Cooking beans in a slow cooker requires pre-soaking by either of the two methods described in "To Soak or Not To Soak the Bean . . . and How," followed by 5 to 6 hours of cooking at high heat, or 10 to 12 hours at low heat.

Handling the Leftovers

"A bean saved is a bean earned."

Cooked beans spoil very quickly at room temperature or warmer; therefore, it is wise to refrigerate leftovers as soon as possible. Bean dishes will keep nicely in the refrigerator for several days, and even more nicely in a freezer. When reheating them, use very low heat, since they burn easily; using a double boiler for this purpose is advisable.

Basic Broth

"The bean is worthy of its broth."

When a recipe calls for vegetable broth, one can use the

liquor from canned or cooked vegetables or beans, or a vegetable bouillon cube. When none of these is available, one can prepare one's own broth.

The following broth can be made in advance and, if stored in the refrigerator, can be used a week or more as the liquid base for bean dishes or soups:

3 large unpeeled potatoes, quartered
    (peelings add a lot of flavour)
1 large onion, quartered
2 carrots, cut in large pieces
3 stalks celery, cut in large pieces
1 large sprig parsley
1 bay leaf
10–15 garlic cloves
2 1/2 qt water

Simmer over a low flame for one hour or pressure cook for 10 minutes. Strain. Add salt to taste.

A shortcut to more flavour for your bean dishes is to put a few vegetables in large chunks right into your cooker with whatever ingredients the recipe calls for, and remove them when the cooking is done.

Basic Bean Sprouts

"One good bean deserves another."

There is no cheaper source of fresh vitamin-rich salad vegetables than sprouts (3 tbsp of alfalfa seeds, for instance, will produce one quart of sprouts). Sprouts are also palatable in sandwiches, soups, pancakes, omelets, and vegetable dishes.

Alfalfa seeds, chickpeas, lentils, mung beans, or soybeans can be used for this purpose. Soak 3 tbsp seeds overnight. Drain. Place in a quart jar; screw lid on lightly. Put in an unlighted oven, or some other dark, draughtless place where the temperature is relatively constant (68-70°). Rinse and drain three times a day (before meals, say) by simply inverting a strainer over the mouth of the jar, draining the water, and then, while holding the strainer tightly over the jar, putting the jar once more in an upright position. (Or use a bean sprouter, which eliminates the need for the rinsing and draining process.) Within three to five days the sprouts will be ready to eat.

Each type of bean sprout has an optimum length for harvesting:

alfalfa sprouts	about 1 inch long
chickpeas	1/2 to 3/4 inch long
mung beans	1 1/2 to 2 1/2 inches
soybeans*	1/2 to 1 inch
lentils	no longer than 1 inch

Rinse and drain the sprouts when they have reached their optimum length and store in a covered container in the refrigerator. They will keep from three to five days.

Whenever possible, sprouted seed should be used without cooking for full retention of all nutrients. They are extremely high in vitamins C, B, and E, as well as being a good source of protein.

*Soybean sprouts need to be parboiled for 10 minutes before use in a salad; this is essential for full digestibility.

Basic Tofu

"East, West, Bean is Best."

Now available in supermarkets and in health food shops, tofu or soybean curd is the "health food" par excellence, being high in assimilable protein, low in calories, low in saturated fats, high in vitamin and mineral content, and easily digestible! But while it is instantly edible, its bland taste requires that it be combined with other foods and flavours (sweet and savoury) to make it tasty.

Since legume and grain proteins, possessing opposite strengths and weaknesses in protein components, complement each other so beautifully in boosting the amount of protein assimilable by the body, it is best to learn to use tofu and grains together, or at least to combine both tofu and grain dishes at the same meal.

Including tofu in one's diet can be very easy to do, once one gets the knack. Here are a few ways:

Combine 1/2 cup diced tofu with 1 cup cooked oatmeal; heat through.

Combine diced tofu with peanut or other nut butters and use as a sandwich spread.

Blend tofu with dried onion soup mix to taste and serve as a dip with crackers.

Use in diced or mashed form with your favourite spaghetti or curry sauce (instead of meat).

Add diced tofu to any canned soup just before serving.

Mash and mix with scrambled eggs.

Combine with sautéed green peppers and onions seasoned with soy sauce and serve over cooked rice.

Combine with canned or fresh fruit and serve with biscuits or cake.

Combine with mixed greens and serve with garlic bread for a well-balanced lunch.

As soon as tofu is brought home, it should be removed from its container, drained, placed in a glass jar, and put in the refrigerator. It will stay fresh this way for two or three days. After that it can be kept in salty water for another four or five days; the salt will, however, take away some of its delicate flavour. It can also be freshened by being placed in a pan of scalding hot water for 2 to 3 minutes.

"Plan your wardrobe around Basic Bean."

2 BEAN SOUPS

Bean on Bean Soup

SERVES FOUR

Serve with French bread and a salad consisting of finely sliced
cabbage, shredded carrots, and sliced black olives with a wine
vinegar and olive oil dressing.

2 cups soy beans
7 cups Basic Broth
  (pp. 11 –12)
1 1/2 cups minced onions
4 minced garlic cloves

4 tbsp sesame or peanut oil
3 tomatoes, cut in eighths
Miso

Soak beans (pp. 5–6). Drain.

Sauté onions and garlic in the oil.

Combine all ingredients except tomatoes and miso.

Pressure cook (pp. 6–10).

Add tomatoes and simmer for 2–3 minutes.

Add miso to taste.

Curried Lima Bean Soup

SERVES FOUR

Serve corn on the cob as a second course and fresh cantaloupe or grapefruit as dessert.

2 cups dried lima beans
7 cups water or Basic Broth
   (pp. 11–12)
1 tbsp oil
4 whole cloves
4 peppercorns
1 bay leaf

1 tsp chili powder
1 tbsp curry powder
2 cups chopped onions
1 cup sliced carrots
3 tbsp butter or margarine
1/2 tsp paprika

Soak the beans (pp. 5–6). Drain.

Add all ingredients except curry powder, butter, and paprika. (The whole spices can be put into a metal tea ball or spoon for easy removal later.)

Pressure cook (pp. 6–10).

Purée, using a food mill.

Melt butter, add curry powder and paprika, and add to the soup. Dilute with water to desired consistency.

Ecossoise

SERVES FOUR

Serve cold on a hot day, each bowl decorated with chopped parsley, chives, or mint.

2 cups Great Northern beans
6 cups water or Basic Broth
(pp. 11–12)
2 medium onions
2 garlic cloves
2 stalks celery

1/2 cup olive oil
Juice of 2 lemons
1 bunch scallions, chopped
4 tbsp chopped fresh parsley
or 2 tbsp dried parsley

Rinse and soak beans (pp. 5–6). Drain.

Pressure cook (pp. 6–10) with onions, garlic, and celery (left whole).

Place cooker under cold water to reduce pressure.

Remove vegetables.

Add olive oil, lemon juice, parsley, and scallions.

Blend thoroughly, adding water if necessary, until silken smooth.

Add salt and pepper to taste.

East Indian Lentil Soup

Purpoo Mulligatunny

SERVES FOUR

Good with whole wheat toast and a finger salad of fresh carrots,
celery, radishes, and zucchini served with a dip of tofu blended
with dried onion soup mix to taste.

2 cups lentils
7 cups water or Basic Broth
   (pp. 11–12)
2 tbsp oil
1 tbsp raw rice
1/2 cup minced onions
1 minced garlic clove

1/3 tsp (or more) dried ground
   chili peppers
2 tsp Indian curry powder
1 tbsp lemon juice

Combine all ingredients except lemon juice.

Pressure cook (pp. 6—10).

Add lemon juice and salt to taste.

Add a dollop of butter or margarine to each bowl.

Eight Bean Soup

SERVES FOUR TO FIVE

Serve with rye toast and a fruit compote made of peeled apricots, diced tart apples, and a dash of Angostura Bitters.

1/4 cup each of red beans, soup peas, lima beans, pinto beans, navy beans, lentils, green split peas, and garbanzos
7 cups water or Basic Broth (pp. 11–12)
1/4 cup raw rice or barley
4 tbsp oil
1 cup chopped onion
1/2 cup chopped green pepper

1/2 cup chopped celery
1/2 cup chopped carrots
1/2 cup chopped parsley
1 minced garlic clove
2 bay leaves
1/4 tsp each powdered marjoram and thyme
1/2 tsp each basil and rosemary leaves
1 cup canned or fresh tomatoes

Soak the beans (pp. 5–6). Drain.

Add the rest of the ingredients *except tomatoes* and pressure cook (pp. 6–10).

Add tomatoes and water to make desired consistency. Add salt and freshly ground pepper to taste. Heat thoroughly.

French Split Pea Soup

Potage Aux Fines Herbes

SERVES FOUR

Serve with garlic bread and a fruit compote consisting of diced oranges, bananas, apples, orange juice, and honey, topped with toasted sunflower seeds.

2 cups dried yellow split peas
7 cups water or Basic Broth
  (pp. 11–12)
4 peppercorns
2 chopped carrots
1 chopped celery stalk
1 cup chopped potato

1/2 cup chopped onion
3 tbsp oil
1/4 tsp each powdered
  marjoram and thyme
1/2 tsp each oregano and
  savory leaves
1 bay leaf

Combine all ingredients and pressure cook (pp. 6–10).

Dilute and/or blend to desired consistency and add salt to taste.

Italian Lentil Soup with Spinach

SERVES FOUR

Serve with corn bread and a bean sprout/shredded car-
rot/hazelnut salad.

2 cups lentils
7 cups water or Basic Broth
 (pp. 11–12)
1/2 cup sliced onions
1/4 cup olive oil

1/2 lb fresh spinach *or* 1 pkg
 frozen chopped spinach
2 tbsp lemon juice
4 tbsp margarine or butter

Fry onions over gentle heat in olive oil until golden; add to lentils
and water.

Pressure cook (pp. 6–10).

Add the spinach, chopped, and simmer without pressure for 15
minutes.

Add the lemon juice. Dilute the soup with hot water to desired
consistency.

Serve with a small dollop of butter in each bowl.

Jim's Pea Soup

SERVES FOUR

Serve with a salad made of bean sprouts, finely sliced cabbage, walnuts, and a dressing consisting of 4 parts tofu, 2 parts oil, 1 part lemon juice, and honey to taste.

2 cups dry soup peas
7 cups water or Basic Broth
  (pp. 11–12)
3 sliced carrots
1 cup chopped onion
1/2 cup chopped celery

2 potatoes, cut in eighths
2 tsp ground mustard seeds
8 whole cloves
1 tsp chili powder
4 tbsp oil

Soak peas (pp. 5–6). Drain.

Combine with all other ingredients and pressure cook (pp. 6–10).

Add salt and freshly ground pepper to taste.

This soup can also be made in a saucepan with fresh peas.

Kentucky Black Bean Soup

SERVES FOUR TO FIVE

Garnish each serving with a thin round slice of lemon. Complete
the menu with corn bread and a salad consisting of asparagus
and pimento on lettuce with tofu mayonnaise.

7 cups water or Basic Broth (pp. 11–12)	1/8 tsp allspice
2 1/2 cups black beans	1 tbsp Worcestershire sauce
4 tbsp olive oil	1/8 tsp black pepper
1/2 lemon, cut in four pieces	1 cup chopped onions
2 cloves stuck in each lemon piece	1/3 cup sherry (optional)
1/4 tsp nutmeg	2 tbsp butter or margarine
	Lemon slices

Soak beans (pp. 5–6). Drain.

Combine beans with all ingredients except butter and sherry.

Pressure cook (pp. 6–10).

Reduce pressure quickly by placing cooker under cold water
tap.

Remove lemon and cloves.

Purée, using a food mill. Add water to make desired
consistency.

Add sherry, butter, and salt to taste. Heat to boiling point.

Tofu Mayonnaise

1/2 cup olive oil   1 cup tofu
1/4 cup red wine vinegar   Freshly ground pepper
2 garlic cloves

Blend all ingredients, adding salt to taste.

Lebanese Lentil Soup with Rice

Makhlouta

SERVES FOUR

Serve with rye toast and a salad of mixed green pepper slices, pineapple chunks, diced tofu, and a lemon juice dressing on lettuce.

7 cups water or Basic Broth (pp. 11–12)	1/2 cup lentils
1/2 cup chickpeas (garbanzos)	1/2 cup rice
1/4 cup black beans	1/4 cup olive oil
	1/2 cup minced onions
	1 tsp caraway seeds

Soak legumes (pp. 5–6). Drain.

Sauté onions in the olive oil over gentle heat until well browned.

Add onions, along with all of the other ingredients, to the legumes.

Pressure cook (pp. 6–10).

Add salt to taste. Dilute with broth to desired consistency.

Lima Bean Chowder

SERVES FOUR

Garnish each bowl with minced parsley and serve with hard rolls. An accompanying salad might be made of finely sliced cabbage, grated carrots, raisins, toasted sunflower seeds, and a light dressing of 3 parts oil, 1 part vinegar, salt and sugar to taste.

1 cup dried lima beans	4 tbsp margarine or butter
2 cups water or Basic Broth (pp. 11–12)	4 cups stewed tomatoes
	1 1/2 tsp celery salt
1 tbsp oil	1/4 tsp pepper
2 cups finely minced onion	1 tbsp sugar
2 cups raw potatoes cut in large pieces	2 tbsp flour
	1/4 cup minced parsley

Soak beans (pp. 5–6). Drain.

Sauté onions and potatoes in the oil.

Combine water or broth, beans, onions, and potatoes in cooker.

Pressure cook (pp. 6–10). Reduce pressure gradually.

Combine bean mixture with tomatoes, celery salt, pepper, and sugar. Bring to boiling point.

Brown the flour in the butter; add liquid gradually until smooth.

Combine flour and bean mixtures; stir. Simmer five minutes.

Marvy Navy Bean Soup

SERVES THREE

Serve with hard rolls and a cartwheel apple/grapefruit salad dressed with 3 parts oil, 1 part lemon juice, 1 part honey, and a dash of Angostura bitters.

1 cup navy beans	4 peppercorns
6 cups water or Basic Broth	3 tbsp oil
(pp. 11–12)	1/2 tsp mustard
1/2 cup chopped onions	3 tbsp brown sugar
3 cloves	

Soak the beans (pp. 5–6). Drain.

Add the remaining ingredients.

Pressure cook (pp. 6–10).

Remove peppercorns and cloves.

Add salt and pepper to taste.

Mexican Chickpea Soup

Sopa de Garbanzos Campechana

SERVES THREE

The menu might include burritos made with flour tortillas that have been spread with taco sauce, shredded yellow cheese, and sliced black olives, then rolled up and placed in an oiled skillet, covered, and heated over low heat; plus a dessert of fresh diced pears mixed with chopped dates and toasted sunflower seeds. [To toast sunflower seeds put a cup or more seeds in a heavy-bottomed pan on medium heat and stir constantly until they are light brown. A little salt can be added during this process.]

1 cup chickpeas (garbanzos)	1 tsp turmeric
5 cups Basic Broth	3 tbsp butter or margarine
(pp. 11–12)	2 tbsp flour
2 cups chopped onion	

Soak chickpeas (pp. 5–6). Drain.

Sauté onions in butter until golden brown.

Combine chickpeas, onions, turmeric, and broth.

Pressure cook (pp. 6–10).

Purée through a food mill.

Brown the flour with a little oil or butter in a frying pan, and add it to the ingredients. Cook two minutes more. Salt to taste.

Add a dollop of butter to each bowl at serving time.

Minestrone

SERVES FIVE

Serve with plenty of garlic bread and a mixed salad of diced
bananas and tofu, chopped walnuts, lettuce, and a little lemon
juice.

2 cups navy beans	2 cups chopped cabbage
7 cups water or Basic Broth	4 peppercorns
(pp. 11–12)	1 bay leaf
1/2 cup olive oil	2 cups canned tomatoes
2 cups chopped onions	2 zucchini, sliced thin
4 tbsp chopped parsley	2 cups macaroni
1 cup chopped celery	Parmesan cheese

Soak beans (pp. 5–6). Drain.

Sauté onions, parsley, celery, and cabbage in the olive oil.

Combine beans, sautéed vegetables, peppercorns, and bay leaf.

Pressure cook (pp. 6–10).

Add zucchini, macaroni, tomatoes, and boiling water as
necessary.

Simmer 15 minutes. Salt to taste.

Top each serving with a generous amount of Parmesan cheese.

Mulligatawny Soup

SERVES FOUR

Serve with whole wheat toast; and, as a side dish, yoghurt mixed with peeled and thinly sliced cucumbers and sprinkled with cardamom seeds.

2 cups split peas
7 cups water or Basic Broth
  (pp. 11–12)
1/2 cup chopped carrots
1/2 cup chopped celery

1/2 cup chopped onion
2 tsp curry powder
4 tbsp vegetable oil
2 tbsp lemon juice

Combine all ingredients except the lemon juice.

Pressure cook (pp. 6–10).

Add lemon juice and salt and pepper to taste. Dilute with water to right consistency.

Puerto Rican Black Bean Soup

SERVES FOUR

Serve with corn sticks and a tomato and cucumber salad.

2 cups black beans
7 cups water or Basic Broth
   (pp. 11–12)
4 garlic cloves
1 1/2 tsp crushed cumin seeds
   (or 1 tsp powdered cumin)

1 tsp oregano leaves
5 tbsp olive oil
1 cup chopped onions
1/2 cup chopped green
   peppers

Soak beans (pp. 5–6). Drain.

Combine all ingredients.

Pressure cook (pp. 6–10).

Purée through a food mill (optional).

Add salt, pepper, and additional broth or water to taste.

Purée of Lentil Soup with Curry

SERVES FOUR

Serve with poppy seed rolls and a round fruit compote of melon
balls, cherries, and grapes flavoured with fresh grated ginger.

2 cups lentils	2 tbsp vegetable or peanut oil
7 cups water or Basic Broth	3 tsp curry powder
(pp. 11–12)	1/2 cup milk or light cream
1 1/2 cups chopped onions	

Wash the lentils.

Sauté the onions for ten minutes in the oil.

Combine all ingredients except the cream.

Pressure cook (pp. 6–10).

Purée through a food mill.

Add the cream. Heat.

Add salt and freshly ground pepper to taste.

Soup Pea Soup

SERVES THREE

Serve with grilled toast topped with mashed tofu mixed with miso to taste, and raw green pepper and zucchini strips.

3/4 cup dry soup peas   1/2 cup chopped celery
2 bay leaves   2 thinly sliced carrots
6 cups water or Basic Broth   1 tsp basil
   (pp. 11–12)   1/8 tsp pepper
1 potato cut in julienne strips   3 tbsp oil
2/3 cup chopped onion   1/4 cup mushrooms

Soak peas (pp. 5–6). Drain.

Add all ingredients except mushrooms and basil.

Pressure cook (pp. 6–10).

Add remaining ingredients and simmer for a few minutes.

Add salt to taste.

3 BEAN SALADS

American Bean Salad

SERVES SIX

2 cups cooked green beans   3/4 cup thin onion slices
2 cups cooked wax beans   1/2 cup thin green pepper
2 cups cooked kidney beans   slices

Dressing:

3/4 cup sugar   1 tsp salt
2/3 cup white vinegar   1/2 tsp pepper
1/2 cup vegetable oil

Drain beans.

Add onions and peppers.

Marinate in the dressing for at least two hours.

Drain off some of the dressing. Serve on lettuce leaves.

Apple Bean Sprout Salad

SERVES FOUR

Serve with peanut butter-and-tofu sandwiches. (Peanut butter or other nut butter sandwiches become juicier and lighter in texture if the nut butter is mixed in equal parts with mashed tofu. Nutrition and taste are further enhanced with the addition of bean sprouts.)

1/2 cup celery, sliced thin   1 1/2 cups bean sprouts
1/2 cup chopped nuts   1 cup diced apple

Mix all ingredients with a dressing made of:

2 tbsp lemon juice   4 tbsp tofu
1 tbsp honey   Dash salt

Carrot Salad with Tofu

SERVES FOUR

Serve on lettuce.

2 cups coarsely grated carrots	1 tbsp oil
1 tbsp raisins	2 tbsp lemon juice
1 tbsp hazelnuts	1 tbsp honey
4 tbsp tofu	Dash salt

Blend tofu with oil, lemon juice, honey, and salt.

Mix lightly with carrots, raisins, and hazelnuts.

Garbanzo Salad Feast

SERVES THREE

Serve cold on lettuce with French bread and chilled rosé wine.

1 cup dried (or 2 cups canned) chickpeas	4 tbsp tofu
	4 tbsp olive oil
1/4 cup chopped green pepper	2 tbsp white vinegar
	3 tbsp prepared horseradish
1/2 cup chopped celery	

Rinse and soak beans, using 1/2 tsp soda per quart of soaking water (pp. 5–6).

Cook in an open pan for 30 minutes in the soaking water.

Let stand for two hours. Discard soaking water. Add water to cover.

Cook at low heat in a tightly covered pot for one hour or until tender. (This method keeps the skins of the beans intact.)

Cool.

Mix with peppers, celery, and the dressing of tofu, oil, vinegar, and horseradish that have been blended together.

Add salt and freshly ground pepper to taste.

Gentle Lentil Salad

SERVES THREE

Serve with sesame rolls and fresh cantaloupe.

1 cup lentils	1 1/2 tbsp wine vinegar
2 cups water	1 minced raw onion
1 onion stuck with 3 cloves	2 tbsp minced parsley
1 bay leaf	Quartered tomatoes
2 1/2 tbsp olive oil	

Rinse lentils. Pressure cook (pp. 6–10) with onion and bay leaf and 1 tbsp oil until tender but not mushy.

Reduce pressure gradually. Drain.

Marinate until serving time with the oil, vinegar, minced onion, and salt to taste.

Garnish with freshly ground pepper, parsley, and tomatoes, and serve on chopped spinach.

Great Northern Salad

SERVES TWO

Serve on lettuce garnished with tomatoes and sliced cucumbers. Complete the meal with lemon sorbet and almond biscuits.

1 cup Great Northern beans	1/3 cup olive oil
(*or* 2 cups canned beans)	Juice of 1 lemon
3 cups water	2 tbsp chopped parsley
1 medium onion	4 chopped scallions
2 garlic cloves	Tomatoes and cucumbers

Rinse and soak beans, using 1/2 tsp soda per quart of soaking water (pp. 5–6).

Cook in an open pan for 30 minutes in the soaking water.

Let stand for two hours. Discard soaking water. Add onion, whole garlic cloves, and water to cover.

Cook at low heat in a tightly covered pot for one hour or until tender. (This method keeps the skins of the beans intact.)

Drain. Remove onions and garlic.

Combine with olive oil, lemon juice, parsley, and scallions. Add salt and pepper to taste. Marinate in the refrigerator until cold.

Green Bean and Sprout Salad

SERVES FOUR

Serve on lettuce.

2 cups canned (whole or cut)   4 tbsp olive oil
   green beans   2 tbsp wine vinegar
1 cup sliced fresh   1 mashed garlic clove
   mushrooms   2 cups bean sprouts
Salt and ground pepper

Marinate all ingredients except sprouts for two to four hours in refrigerator.

Add sprouts.

Hot Mixed Bean Salad

SERVES FIVE

When serving, garnish with tomatoes and serve with French fried potatoes and hot tomato bouillon made with 1 tbsp lemon juice and 1 tbsp catsup per quart of tomato juice

1/2 cup chickpeas, 1/2 cup   1/4 cup minced parsley
   pinto beans, 1/2 cup red or   1/3 cup olive oil
   kidney beans; or 4 cups   1/4 cup wine vinegar
   canned beans of choice   1/2 tsp salt
7 cups water or Basic Broth   1/4 tsp freshly ground pepper
   (pp. 11–12)   1/4 tsp dry mustard
1 cup thinly sliced celery   2 tomatoes cut in wedges
1 small red onion, thinly sliced

Rinse and soak beans, using 1/2 tsp baking soda per quart of soaking water (pp. 5–6).

Cook in an open pan for 30 minutes in the soaking water.

Let stand for two hours or more. Discard soaking water. Add water to cover.

Cook at low heat in a tightly covered pot for one hour or until tender. (This method keeps the skins of the beans intact.)

Drain. Add prepared vegetables.

Combine oil, vinegar, and seasonings; shake well. Add to salad.

Heat through.

Korean Bean Sprout Salad

Sook Choo Na Mool

SERVES TWO

Serve with Korean Fried Beans (p. 74) and fresh peaches with candied ginger for dessert.

1/4 cup oil
2 tbsp vinegar
2 tbsp soy sauce
1/2 tsp salt
1/2 tsp freshly ground black
    pepper
1 minced garlic clove

1/4 cup finely chopped
    scallions
1/4 cup julienne-cut pimento
2 tbsp ground toasted sesame
    seeds
2 cups bean sprouts

Mix all ingredients except bean sprouts. Chill.

Add bean sprouts and serve immediately.

Mexican Kidney Bean Salad, No. 1

SERVES FOUR

Serve cold on lettuce with avocado slices and cornsticks.

1 cup tomato sauce
1/4 cup chili sauce
1 tsp hot mustard
2 tbsp grated onion
2 tbsp horseradish
1/2 tsp chili powder
1 tsp dried basil

crushed garlic clove
1/4 cup vinegar
1/4 tsp salt
1/4 tsp Tabasco
2 tbsp olive oil
2 cups cooked kidney beans
(available canned)

Combine all ingredients except beans and oil and simmer for 10 minutes.

Blend with the oil and add the beans.

Marinate for two hours or more.

Mexican Kidney Bean Salad, No. 2

Frijoles Ensalada

SERVES FOUR

Serve on lettuce with tomato wedges, corn chips, and guacamole.

2 cups cooked kidney beans   12 pitted black olives, sliced
    (available canned)   1 tbsp vinegar
1 green pepper, chopped   1 crushed garlic clove
1/2 cup chopped red onion   1 tbsp oil
1 tbsp diced pimento   1/8 tsp chili powder
    (optional)   1/2 tsp oregano

Toss all ingredients until well mixed. Marinate at least two hours.

Guacamole

2 ripe avocados   2 canned green chili peppers,
2–3 tbsp chopped white   cut in 1/2 inch squares
    onion   1/2 tsp salt
3 tbsp lemon juice   Freshly ground pepper
1/2 finely chopped garlic clove

Peel and mash avocados (or put in a blender).

Add remaining ingredients.

Mushroom and Bean Sprout Salad

SERVES THREE

Serve in bowls over hot cooked rice, or as a conventional salad
with lettuce.

2 cups bean sprouts
1 cup sliced fresh
   mushrooms
1/4 cup chopped scallions
2 tbsp oil

1 tbsp soy sauce
1 tsp vinegar
1 tsp Accent
1 crushed garlic clove

Combine oil, soy sauce, vinegar, Accent, and garlic.

Mix with chilled vegetables and serve immediately.

Soy Joy Salad

SERVES SIX

Serve on lettuce garnished with scallions, toasted sunflower
seeds, and tomatoes. Sesame rolls and cold peppermint tea
could complete the menu.

2 cups soybeans   2–3 stalks celery
6 cups water   3 garlic cloves
2 onions   2 bay leaves
2 carrots   1 tbsp oil

Rinse and soak beans (pp. 5–6). Discard soaking water.

Pressure cook (pp. 6–10) with other ingredients, adding the
vegetables whole or cut up just enough to fit into the pressure
cooker.

Reduce pressure gradually.

Remove vegetables. Drain. (Save liquor for Basic Broth.)

Combine beans with enough Italian dressing to cover, and
marinate in the refrigerator until cold.

4 BEAN SANDWICHES, SPREADS, AND SUCH

Amarillo Taco

SERVES FOUR

Serve on buns, toast, or as a filling for tacos. Cooked down or dried out further, it can be used as a sandwich spread.

1 cup soybeans
1 cup garbanzos
5 cups water
1 package dried onion soup
   mix
2 tbsp chili powder

4 tbsp oil
1/2 hot green pepper (optional)
Tabasco Sauce

Soak beans (pp. 5–6). Drain.

Add all ingredients except Tabasco. Pressure cook (pp. 6–10).

Mash with potato masher until desired consistency is obtained. Cook down to proper thickness if necessary.

Season with Tabasco to taste.

Cosmopolitan Bean Cakes

SERVES FOUR TO SIX

Serve with a salad consisting of bean sprouts, garlic, scallions, tomatoes, and a dressing of 2 tbsp wine vinegar, 1/2 cup olive oil, salt, and freshly ground pepper. A fruit cup of pineapple, coconut, and dates could finish off the meal.

2 cups cornmeal	1 cup cooked kidney beans
1/2 tsp salt	4 tsp miso (or to taste)
2 cups boiling water	

Combine cornmeal and salt.

Add boiling water and stir constantly until dough becomes stiff.

Divide into 8 equal portions and cool.

Divide each portion into two and pat into flat thin cakes about 2 inches in diameter. If mixture is sticky, dip spatula in cold water.

Mash or grind beans and mix well with the miso.

Place 2 tbsp of the mixture on half of the cakes, spreading it evenly.

Press edges together to seal.

Fry over low heat in hot oil until each side is golden brown. Turn only once.

Crêpes Suzanna

SERVES FOUR TO SIX

These can also be fried as small pancakes. Or filled with curried or creamed vegetables and served as an entrée.

1/2 cup yellow split peas	2 tsp lemon juice
3/4 cup rice	1 tsp salt
1 1/2 tbsp oil	

Soak peas and rice in separate bowls for eight to ten hours. Drain.

Begin heating griddle or skillet at high heat.

Add 1/2 cup water to the peas; blend for approximately 1 minute or until smooth.

Remove pea solution to a bowl.

Add 1 1/4 cups water to the rice; blend for approximately 1 1/2 minutes or until smooth.

Add pea solution to the rice solution; add oil, lemon juice, and salt and blend briefly.

Oil skillet thoroughly; pour off excess oil.

With one hand hold skillet off the fire; with the other hand pour a thin stream of batter into the surface of the skillet, beginning at the centre, and turning the skillet about to spread the mixture evenly. Pour off excess batter to keep the crêpe as thin as possible.

Bake without turning until the bottom of the crêpe is golden brown and can be turned over in one piece with a spatula. If the batter is thin enough the crêpe will need to be fried on one side only.

Sprinkle with lemon juice and icing sugar; roll, and place in a warm oven until serving time.

Egg Rolls

MAKES FOUR TO SIX EGG ROLLS

Serve as an appetizer or with soup for a simple lunch.

2 cups chopped Chinese cabbage	1 tbsp grated fresh ginger root
1 garlic clove	Soy or tamari sauce
1 cup chopped bean sprouts	Cayenne pepper
1 small onion or 3–4 scallions	4 to 6 egg roll "skins" (now
1 cup mashed tofu	available at many supermarkets)

Combine chopped vegetables and tofu; fry briefly in a
teaspoonful of sesame or peanut oil to reduce moisture
content.

Season with soy or tamari sauce, and a pinch of cayenne.

To make rolls, arrange 3–4 tbsp of the filling along one side of
the skin. Fold over the outer ends of the skins about 1/2 inch
before rolling the skin over the filling. Pack the filling as tightly as
possible. Paste the roll together with a little water.

Fry in hot deep oil (370°) until skin is crisp, bubbly, and brown.

Garbanzo Sandwich Spread

SERVES FOUR

Serve on pumpernickel or rye bread with lettuce.

1 cup cooked or canned garbanzos	1/4 tsp powdered thyme
2 tbsp lemon juice	1/2 tsp basil leaves
2 tbsp yoghurt	1/2 tsp oregano leaves
	1 crushed garlic clove

Mash the garbanzos.

Combine with other ingredients and salt to taste.

This spread will keep in the refrigerator several days.

Lebanese Garbanzo Dip

SERVES SIX TO SEVEN

1/4 cup olive oil
1/4 cup lemon juice
2 cups cooked
   garbanzos

1/2 cup sesame seeds *or* 1/2
   cup sesame butter [tahini]
1 crushed garlic clove
   (optional)

Toast sesame seeds by tossing them in a heavy pan over
medium heat until golden brown.

Grind the sesame seeds fine in a blender; add 1/2 of the oil and
juice; blend until smooth.

Add the garbanzos and rest of the oil and juice, a little at a time.

Add a little salt to taste. Add water to the consistency desired.

Lentil Burgers

SERVES FOUR

Serve with catsup or steak sauce.

2 cups cooked lentils
1 cup whole wheat bread
   crumbs
1/2 cup wheat germ (optional)

1/2 tsp salt
1/4 cup grated onion
1/2 tsp celery seeds (optional)
3 tbsp oil

Mash the lentils slightly. Mix with other ingredients.

Form into patties. Coat with crumbs.

Fry on both sides until brown.

Lima Bean Sandwiches

SERVES FOUR TO FIVE

Can be served as cold sandwiches or grilled as open-face
sandwiches.

1 cup cooked lima beans	3 tbsp brown sugar
1/2 cup crushed nuts or 1/2	1 tbsp oil
cup ground pumpkin seeds	1/8 tsp cinnamon

Grind or mash lima beans.

Add other ingredients.

Soy Sandwiches

SERVES FOUR TO FIVE

Serve with whole wheat bread and radishes.

1 cup cooked soybeans,   2 tbsp oil
   drained well   Grated fresh ginger
2 tbsp Kikkoman soy sauce   Raisins
   (Japanese)

Mash soybeans or put through a grinder.

Add soy sauce and oil.

Add ginger and raisins to taste.

Soybean Sandwich Spread

SERVES FOUR TO FIVE

Serve on whole wheat bread with a tomato and bean sprout salad.

1 cup cooked soybeans   2 tbsp mayonnaise
1/4 cup green olives with   1 tbsp chopped scallions
   pimentos

Chop or grind soybeans, olives, and scallions together. Add other ingredients and salt to taste.

Soyburgers Supreme

SERVES THREE

Serve with lettuce, tomato slices, and pickles on toasted buns.

(These burgers can be made in advance, placed between pieces of wax paper, and frozen until ready to fry.)

1 cup soybeans	1/2 tsp salt
4 cups Basic Broth	1 tbsp oil
(pp. 11–12)	1 cup quick-cooking oatmeal
1/4 tsp chili powder	2 tbsp soy sauce (preferably
1/4 tsp dry mustard	Kikkoman)
1/8 tsp cayenne or dried chili	1 cup coarsely chopped onion
peppers	

Rinse and soak soybeans (pp. 5–6). Drain.

Add four cups Basic Broth. If no Basic Broth is available, add five cups water and the following ingredients (whole): one potato, 1 onion, 1 carrot, 1 stalk celery, 1 garlic clove.

Add chili powder, mustard, cayenne, salt, and oil.

Pressure cook (pp. 6–10).

Reduce pressure, drain soybeans well, remove whole vegetables.

Toss the oatmeal in a skillet over high heat until lightly toasted.

Add oatmeal, onions, and soy sauce to soybeans. Mash only until mixture begins to hold together.

Form firm balls between the palms of your hands, then flatten out to form burgers. Fry in a little oil or margarine for three to four minutes. For a crisper, firmer texture, dip each burger into flour before frying.

Tahini and Miso Spread

1/2 cup tahini (sesame butter)   1 tbsp miso (or more to taste)

Mix well and dilute with a little water or lemon juice if a dip consistency is desired.

For sandwiches spread thickly on whole wheat bread and cover with bean sprouts instead of lettuce.

USA Paté

Use as a dip or combine with tofu or cheese as a sandwich spread.

1 cup cooked soybeans	1/4 cup vegetable or olive oil
2 cups finely chopped (unpeeled) eggplant	1 tbsp tomato paste
	2 tbsp lemon juice
1 cup finely chopped green peppers	1/4 tsp cayenne pepper

Fry the peppers and eggplant at low heat for about 15 minutes.

Purée soybeans, peppers, and eggplant in food mill.

Add tomato paste, lemon juice, and cayenne pepper and salt to taste.

5 STOVETOP BEANPOTS

Armenian Lentil Pilau

Moujet Derreh

SERVES THREE

Serve with fried eggplant and a cucumber and yoghurt salad.

1 cup lentils	1 tbsp oil
1 1/2 cups bulgur (parboiled cracked wheat)	1/2 tsp salt
	1/4 lb butter
6 cups water	1 medium onion, sliced

Rinse lentils.

Combine lentils, bulgur, water, oil, and salt.

Pressure cook (pp. 6–10).

Sauté onions in butter until they are *golden brown*. Use gentle heat and stir constantly.

Reduce pressure on lentils by placing cooker under cold water.

Serve lentils with a spoonful of onions on each serving.

Garnish with paprika and slivered almonds (optional).

Blackeyes with Marjoram

SERVES THREE

Serve with cooked greens flavored with soy sauce, vinegar, and butter, and topped with thinly sliced oranges.

1 1/2 cups black-eyed peas	1 tsp salt
3 cups water	1 dried red pepper pod
1 bay leaf	1 tsp powdered marjoram
1/2 cup chopped onion	2 minced garlic cloves
3 tbsp raw rice	3 tbsp oil

Wash peas thoroughly.

Pressure cook with rest of ingredients (pp. 6–10).

Chili sin Carne

SERVES THREE TO FOUR

Serve with grilled cheese toast and Apple Bean Sprout Salad (p. 39).

1 1/2 cups kidney beans	1/4 tsp dried ground chilis
3 cups water	1/8 tsp cayenne
4 cups canned tomatoes	1/2 cup chopped onions
1 tbsp cumin seed or 2 1/2 tsp cumin powder	1/2 cup chopped green peppers
3 minced garlic cloves	6 tbsp oil

Wash and soak (pp. 5–6) beans. Drain.

Sauté onions and peppers in oil.

Combine all ingredients and pressure cook (pp. 6–10).

Let pressure come down gradually.

Add salt to taste.

Chow Bean Sprouts and Peppers

SERVES THREE

Serve on hot boiled rice and top with toasted cashews or almonds. Serve with egg rolls (p. 54).

2 tbsp vegetable oil
1/2 tsp salt
3 cups green peppers, sliced
1 qt alfalfa or mung bean
    sprouts
2 hot chili peppers (optional)

1 slice ginger
1/4 cup vegetable stock or
    Basic Broth (pp. 11–12)
1 tsp sherry
1/2 tsp Accent

Heat oil in a wok or heavy skillet until smoking hot.

Add salt and green peppers and stir for 1 minute.

Add bean sprouts, peppers, and ginger and stir for another minute.

Add broth and cover for 3 minutes.

Add the rest of the ingredients and heat through.

Cuban Rice with Black Beans

Arroz con Frijoles

SERVES FOUR TO SIX

Accompanying dishes could be a mixed green salad and assorted fruit for dessert.

1 1/4 cups black beans
7 cups water or Basic Broth
  (pp. 11–12)
1 large onion, sliced
2 garlic cloves
2 thinly sliced green peppers

1 bay leaf
1 tsp pepper
2 cloves
1 1/2 cups long grain natural
  rice
1/2 cup olive oil

Soak beans (pp. 5–6). Drain.

Combine beans, rice, bay leaf, cloves, and half of the garlic, onion, peppers, and oil.

Add the water and pressure cook (pp. 6–10).

Reduce pressure gradually.

In remaining oil, fry remaining onion, garlic, and peppers until transparent. Add pepper and salt to taste.

Serve the fried vegetables over the beans and rice sprinkled with Tabasco sauce.

East Indian Curried Greens

SERVES THREE

A colourful dish! Serve with hot rice or hash brown potatoes, buttered carrots, and yoghurt mixed with fresh or canned apricots.

1 cup green split peas
3 cups water
1 tsp salt
1 tbsp oil
1 tsp Indian curry powder
1 tsp grated fresh ginger (or 1/4 tsp powdered ginger)
3 medium onions, chopped

1 large garlic clove, minced
2 cups chopped kale, chard, spinach, mustard greens, collards, or comfrey
3 cinnamon sticks
4 whole cloves
3 tbsp margarine or butter

Rinse the peas.

Add water, salt, oil, and curry powder, and pressure cook (pp. 6–10) for 15–20 minutes.

Place cooker under cold water to reduce pressure.

Add the onion, ginger, garlic, and greens.

Cover and boil without pressure until vegetables are tender and the mixture is fairly dry (guard against scorching).

Melt the butter in a skillet, add the cinnamon sticks and cloves, and the pea mixture.

Fry over low heat until butter is absorbed. Remove cloves and cinnamon.

East Indian Pilau

SERVES THREE TO FOUR

Serve with buttered cauliflower, garnished with cayenne, and a yoghurt and cucumber salad sprinkled with a few cardamom seeds.

1 cup dried soup peas	1/4 tsp cinnamon
3 cups water or Basic Broth	1/4 tsp powdered ginger
(pp. 11–12)	1 tsp turmeric
1/2 cup brown rice	1 cup chopped onion
4 tbsp butter	1/4 cup slivered almonds
1/2 tsp thyme	(optional)
1/4 tsp allspice	1/4 cup golden raisins
1/2 tsp salt	(optional)

Wash and soak peas (pp. 5–6). Drain.

Pressure cook peas and rice (pp. 6–10).

Meanwhile, fry onions with spices until tender.

Reduce pressure gradually.

Combine peas, rice, and onion mixture and place on low heat until all liquid is absorbed.

Garnish each serving with almonds and raisins.

Foo Yung American

SERVES THREE

Serve with fried rice and steamed broccoli.

Make the following sauce first:

1 tsp cornstarch   1 tsp vinegar
1 tsp sugar   1/2 cup Basic Broth
2 tsp soy sauce   (pp. 11–12) or water

Cook over low heat until thick. Keep warm until ready to serve.

4 eggs, well beaten (or 2 eggs   1/2 minced garlic clove
   and 1/2 cup mashed tofu)   1/4 tsp salt
1 cup bean sprouts   1/8 tsp pepper
1/3 cup thinly sliced scallions   2 tbsp vegetable oil
1/8 cup thinly sliced celery

Combine all ingredients except oil.

Heat the oil in a large frying pan; pour in the egg mixture by the tablespoonful to make small cakes.

Turn each one once, cooking until lightly browned.

Place on a hot plate and cover with hot sauce.

Garbanzos with Spices

SERVES FOUR

Serve with hot boiled natural rice and plain yoghurt mixed with apricots and garnished with crushed cardamom seeds.

4 cups cooked garbanzo beans	1/4 tsp ground red chili peppers
3 tbsp butter or margarine	2 chopped tomatoes
1 1/2 cups chopped onion	1/4 tsp powdered ginger
1 1/2 tsp turmeric	2 tbsp minced parsley
1/2 tsp cumin seed, crushed	1 cup bean broth or Basic Broth (pp. 11–12)

Sauté the onion for 10 minutes at low heat.

Mix in spices and garbanzos.

Cook over low heat for 5 minutes.

Add the tomatoes, salt, and broth.

Cook over low heat for 10 minutes or until most of the liquid has evaporated.

Sprinkle with the parsley.

Hot Lentil Curry

SERVES FOUR

Serve on hot boiled rice with a generous serving of the tomato sauce (heated) on top to lend the curry both taste and colour. Serve with a side dish of canned pears and diced tofu flavoured with fresh grated ginger and lemon juice.

1 cup lentils
2 cups water or Basic Broth (pp. 11–12)
2 tsp oil
4 tbsp butter or margarine
1 tbsp ground cumin seeds, or 2 tsp powdered cumin
2 tsp turmeric powder
1/2 tsp dry mustard

4 cups peeled and cubed eggplant
1 cup chopped onion
1 cup chopped green peppers
1 fresh or canned green chili pepper
Tomato sauce
Worcestershire sauce

Rinse and pressure cook lentils with broth and oil (pp. 6–10).

Fry cumin, turmeric, and mustard in the butter.

Add the eggplant, onion, green and hot peppers and fry.

Add 2 cups water and stew until vegetables are tender.

Add lentil mixture, salt, and Worcestershire sauce to taste. Mixture should be quite juicy.

Iranian Stew

Ash e Mast

SERVES THREE TO FOUR

5 cups water	2 tsp crushed dried coriander
5 tbsp oil	2 pkg frozen chopped spinach
4 large onions	*or* 2 lb fresh chopped
1/3 cup dried yellow split peas	spinach
1 cup rice	2 qt yoghurt
2 tbsp fresh chopped parsley	1 tsp dried mint leaves
1 tbsp fresh chopped chives	

Slice the onions and sauté in the oil, stirring until well browned.

Combine the water, peas, rice, coriander, and 1/4 of the fried onions.

Pressure cook for 15 minutes (pp. 6–10).

Reduce pressure under cold water.

Add the chopped greens and cook until tender.

Add the yoghurt and heat through without allowing mixture to boil.

Top each serving with some of the remaining fried onions and a pinch of dried mint.

Italian Macaroni and Beans

Pasta e Fagioli

SERVES THREE

Serve with garlic bread, red wine, and mushroom and bean sprout salad (p. 47).

1 cup kidney beans	1/2 tsp basil
1/2 cup lentils	2 cups stewed tomatoes
4 cups water	1 8-oz can tomato sauce
1/2 cup chopped onion	4 tbsp olive oil
1/3 cup chopped celery	1/4 tsp pepper
1/3 cup chopped parsley	2/3 cup pasta
1/4 cup chopped mint	Parmesan cheese, grated

Wash and soak beans (pp. 5–6). Drain.

Sauté onion, garlic, and celery.

Combine all ingredients except pasta and cheese. Pressure cook (pp. 6–10). Reduce pressure gradually.

Add pasta (shells, bows, etc.). Simmer until pasta is done (about 10–12 minutes).

Place in a casserole; sprinkle liberally with Parmesan; heat in oven until ready to serve.

Japanese Red Beans with Rice

Seki Han

SERVES TWO TO THREE

Serve with cooked spinach flavoured with equal parts oil, soy sauce, and vinegar, and garnished with toasted sesame seeds and mandarin oranges.

4 cups water or Basic Broth (pp. 11–12)	2 cups cooked rice
1 1/2 cups red beans	2 tbsp sherry or sake or 1 tbsp wine vinegar
3 tbsp soy sauce	

Wash and soak beans (pp. 5–6). Drain.

Pressure cook (pp. 6–10).

Reduce pressure gradually. Drain.

Combine lightly with rice, soy sauce, and wine.

Cover and cook over low heat until dry, about 5 minutes.

Korean Fried Beans

Pah Jook

SERVES THREE

Serve with hot rice that has been mixed with sautéed green onions, garlic, bean sprouts, and toasted ground sesame seeds. Add soy sauce to taste. For a Korean feast, add *Sook Choo Na Mool* (p. 44), a Korean bean sprout salad.

1 cup red or kidney beans	1 garlic clove
3 cups water	2 cups cooked rice
1 cup chopped onion	1/2 cup Basic Broth
1/3 cup sesame or vegetable oil	(pp. 11–12)
	1/2 tsp dried ground chilis

Rinse and soak beans (pp. 5–6). Drain.

Pressure cook (pp. 6–10) with garlic, onion, 1 tbsp oil, and 3 cups water.

Mash well or purée through a food mill.

Heat the remainder of the oil in a skillet; add the beans and cook for five minutes.

Stir in the rice, broth, and chilis. Cook 5 minutes.

Lentil Spaghetti

SERVES FOUR

Serve over cooked spaghetti with grated cheese on top; and a mixed green salad of green peppers, cabbage, lettuce, and scallions.

1 cup chopped onion
2 minced garlic cloves
2 tbsp olive oil
1 cup lentils
2 cups water or Basic Broth
   (pp. 11–12)
1 small can mushrooms
   (optional)

1 6-oz can tomato paste
1/2 tsp oregano leaves
1/4 tsp basil leaves
1/4 tsp cayenne pepper
Grated Parmesan cheese
Whole wheat spaghetti

Sauté onions and garlic in olive oil.

Add to lentils and broth.

Pressure cook (pp. 6–10).

Add tomato paste, mushrooms, spices, and cayenne pepper.

Add salt to taste.

Liberation Black-eyed Peas

SERVES THREE TO FOUR

Serve immediately with buttered spinach, cornmeal muffins, and watermelon.

2 cups black-eyed peas	3/4 cup tofu, mashed
4 cups water or Basic Broth (pp. 11–12)	1 tbsp wine vinegar
	1 tsp chili powder
4 tbsp vegetable oil	1 minced garlic clove

Wash black-eyed peas well.

Pressure cook without soaking with broth and oil (pp. 6–10).

Drain.

Add the remaining ingredients.

Lima and Green Bean Extraordinaire

SERVES THREE

Serve with Apple Bean Sprout Salad (p. 39) and toasted English muffins.

1 cup dry lima beans	2 cups fresh or frozen green
3 1/2 cups water	beans
1 bay leaf	1 tsp salt
2 minced garlic cloves	2 tbsp lemon juice
4 tbsp olive oil	

Wash and soak limas (pp. 5–6). Drain.

Add all ingredients except green beans and lemon juice.

Pressure cook (pp. 6–10).

Reduce pressure gradually.

Add green beans. Simmer 5–10 minutes more until beans are tender and most liquid has evaporated.

Add the lemon juice and a healthy grind of fresh pepper.

Place in a casserole and garnish with chopped parsley and onions.

Lima Beans Indiènne

SERVES TWO TO THREE

The menu might include boiled rice flavoured with parsley and butter, and carrots dressed with a brown sugar sauce.

1/3 cup minced onion
1 minced garlic clove
2 tsp grated ginger *or* 1/4 tsp powdered ginger
1 tsp curry powder
2 tbsp butter or oil

2 cups cooked or canned lima beans
3/4 cup yoghurt
1/2 tsp lemon juice
Fried sliced almonds (optional)

Fry onion, garlic, and spices together until onion is transparent.

Add lima beans and cook 5 minutes at low heat.

Add yoghurt and lemon juice and heat without boiling.

Serve garnished with the almonds.

Mexican Refried Beans

Frijoles Refritos

SERVES THREE

Serve with crisp taco shells filled with a mixture of shredded lettuce, diced tofu, and green taco sauce.

2 cups washed pinto beans	2 tsp oil
5 cups water	1/2 cup butter or margarine
1 large onion, chopped	1 tsp salt

Soak the beans (pp. 5–6).

Add the chopped onion and oil and pressure cook (pp. 6–10). Reduce pressure.

Add the butter and salt, and mash with a potato masher until all the butter is absòrbed.

Heat over low heat to desired dryness.

Northern Red Ragout

SERVES THREE

Serve with tomatoes stewed with soybean sprouts and, to complete the red motif, red apple salad and raspberry pudding.

1/2 cup Great Northern beans	1/4 tsp oregano leaves
1/2 cup red beans	1 tsp salt
6 cups water or Basic Broth	3 tbsp olive oil
(pp. 11–12)	2 tbsp pearl barley
1/2 tsp turmeric powder	2 tbsp cracked wheat or rice
1/2 tsp basil leaves	1 dried red chili

Wash and soak (pp. 5–6) the beans. Drain.

Combine all ingredients and pressure cook (pp. 6–10).

The table could be decorated with a bowl of pomegranates, red onions, and apples if one were celebrating a "red letter" day!

Pink Beans with Herbs

SERVES THREE

Serve with hot French bread, chilled white wine, and a Waldorf salad of apples, walnuts, celery, and a honey/tofu dressing on lettuce.

5 cups water or Basic Broth (pp. 11–12)

2 cups pink beans, or pintos

1/2 cup olive oil

1/2 cup butter

2 tbsp lemon juice

1/2 cup chopped chives or scallions

1/4 tsp powdered oregano

1/4 tsp powdered thyme

1/2 tsp basil leaves

1 tsp rosemary leaves

Wash and soak beans (pp. 5–6). Drain.

Pressure cook (pp. 6–10) with 1 tbsp oil and water or Basic Broth.

Reduce pressure gradually.

Meanwhile, combine remaining ingredients, salt to taste, and cook on low heat for 5 minutes. Add to beans and mix well.

Pinto Chili

SERVES THREE

Serve with lettuce and cheddar cheese tacos.

2 cups pinto beans	1 tbsp cumin seeds
5 cups water	1/2 tsp dried ground chilis (or
4 tbsp oil	more)
3 minced garlic cloves	2 tsp salt

Wash and soak (pp. 5–6) beans in the water.

Add remaining ingredients and pressure cook (pp. 6–10).

Reduce the pressure gradually.

Add flour or water to achieve desired consistency.

Pinto Rarebit

SERVES THREE

Serve on hot toast with a tart fruit salad of fresh pineapple, strawberries, bananas, and oranges.

1 cup pinto beans	1/8 tsp Angostura bitters
3 cups water	(optional)
3 tbsp oil	1/3 cup grated cheddar
2 dried red chilis	cheese
1 cup canned tomatoes	

Wash and soak (pp. 5–6) the beans. Drain.

Pressure cook (pp. 6–10) with water, oil, and chilis.

Bring down pressure under cold water.

Purée in food mill.

Add remaining ingredients. Heat. Salt to taste.

If too liquid, thicken with 2 tsp flour mixed with 1 tbsp melted butter.

Potato Frittata

SERVES TWO

Serve with cold asparagus that has been marinated in 1 part
wine vinegar, 2 parts olive oil, and salt and pepper to taste.

2 cold baked potatoes,   1 tbsp vegetable oil or
  unpeeled   margarine
1 medium onion, sliced thin   A 4–6 oz square of tofu
1/2 medium green pepper,   1 egg (optional)
  sliced thin

Sauté onion, green pepper, and diced potatoes at high heat,
stirring constantly.

Place the tofu on a clean cloth or 2-3 thicknesses of paper
towelling; cover, and press out excess moisture.

Dice tofu.

Lower heat on the vegetable mixture; add tofu and toss lightly.
Add one beaten egg if desired to give a scrambled egg texture.

Serve with tamari or Tabasco sauce.

Soybeans Creole

SERVES TWO

Serve with cabbage, spinach, and lettuce salad with tofu mayonnaise (p. 27) and hot baking-powder biscuits.

2 tbsp olive oil	1 cup stewed tomatoes
2 tbsp chopped onion	1 cup vegetable broth
4 tbsp chopped green pepper	1/2 tsp basil
1 minced garlic clove	1/8 tsp cayenne pepper
3 tbsp whole wheat flour	2 cups cooked soybeans

Sauté onions, peppers, and garlic in oil.

Add flour; mix well.

Add remaining ingredients. Cook 10 minutes.

Salt and pepper to taste.

Swedish Brown Beans

Bruna Bönor

SERVES THREE TO FOUR

Serve with escalloped spinach (p. 98), buttered rice, and cold
"fruit soup."

1 3/4 cups dried brown beans   1/3 cup white vinegar
8 cups water   1/2 cup dark corn syrup
1 tsp baking soda   or treacle
1 1/2 tsp salt   2 tbsp brown sugar

Rinse beans. Cook for 30 minutes, covered, in the water to
which soda has been added.

Turn off heat. Let stand for two hours, covered.

Drain.

Add remaining ingredients and water to barely cover the
mixture.

Cook in a tightly covered pot at minimal heat (no pressure) for
one hour or until tender. (This method tenderizes the bean skins
without breaking them.)

Cold Fruit Soup

1/2 lb prunes
1/2 lb dried apricots and pears
1/2 cup sugar
3 raw apples, pared and diced

1 stick cinnamon
2 tbsp potato starch or
    cornstarch

Wash the dried fruit and soak overnight in 2 qt water.

In the morning add sugar, apples, and cinnamon.

Boil until fruit is tender.

Strain out the fruit, removing prune pits and cinnamon.

Mix the starch with a little cold water and use it to thicken the fruit juice. Boil for a few minutes. Add the fruit.

Cool. Serve with light cream.

Tofu Chow Mein

SERVES TWO TO THREE

Serve on crisp chow mein noodles and sprinkle with tamari sauce. For dessert mix 1 can sliced peaches with 1 box thawed raspberries and 1 tsp grated fresh ginger, and serve with jasmine tea.

1 cup chopped celery	1 1/2 cups cubed tofu
1/2 cup chopped onion	2 tbsp sesame oil
1 minced garlic clove	2 tsp corn or potato starch
1 cup sliced mushrooms	Soy sauce

Sauté celery, onion, and garlic in the oil until crisply tender.

Add mushrooms and tofu and water to cover. Stew 3 minutes.

Mix cornstarch with a little water; add and stir until thickened. Add more cornstarch/water mixture until desired thickness is reached.

Add 2 tsp soy sauce or more to taste.

6 OVEN BEANPOTS

Beanpot with Thyme

SERVES THREE TO FOUR

Serve with garlic toast and a salad of bananas and oranges
sliced in thin rounds with a yoghurt, honey, and grated ginger
dressing.

1 cup pink or pinto beans
1/3 cup navy beans
1/3 cup chickpeas
1/2 cup parboiled cracked
    wheat (bulgur) *or* 1/2 cup
    brown rice
6 cups water
1/4 tsp pepper
1 tsp thyme

1/4 tsp ground dried chili
    peppers
4 sliced carrots
1/3 cup chopped onion
1/2 cup chopped green
    pepper
3 tbsp oil
1/2 cup chopped parsley

Rinse and soak beans (pp. 5–6). Drain.

Sauté onions, green pepper and carrots in the oil.

Combine all ingredients except parsley.

Pressure cook (pp. 6–10).

Reduce pressure gradually. Salt to taste.

Place in a casserole; top with buttered bread crumbs.

Bake for 30 minutes at 325°.

Garnish with liberal quantities of minced parsley.

Beans Italiano

SERVES FOUR TO SIX

Serve this with tomatoes that have been hollowed out, stuffed with a mixture of tomato pulp, tofu, garlic, lemon juice, and chopped mint, dressed with olive oil, and baked at the same time as the beans.

2 cups cooked kidney beans	6 tbsp olive oil
2 cups cooked pinto beans	2 tsp basil leaves
1/2 cup chopped green pepper	1 tsp oregano leaves
1/2 cup chopped onion	2 dried hot red peppers (seeds removed)
4 minced garlic cloves	3 cups zucchini, diced

Sauté pepper, onion, and garlic in the oil.

Combine all ingredients plus salt to taste.

Bake for 30 minutes at 350° in covered casserole.

Cover surface with Parmesan cheese and brown under the grill.

Beans Mexicali

SERVES THREE TO FOUR

Serve with crisp tacos filled with a mixture of shredded cabbage, diced tofu, and green taco sauce.

2 cups red beans
6 cups water or Basic Broth
  (pp. 11–12)
1/3 cup olive oil
1 chopped green pepper
1 crushed garlic clove
1 cup chopped onion

2 cups canned tomatoes
1 tsp chili powder
1/8 tsp thyme
1/2 tsp dry mustard
2 tbsp brown sugar
2 tbsp parsley
1 bay leaf

Rinse and soak beans (pp. 5–6). Drain.

Pressure cook with broth and 1 tbsp oil (pp. 6–10). Reduce pressure gradually.

Fry onion, peppers, and garlic in the rest of the oil.

Combine all ingredients in a casserole, adding salt to taste.

Bake, uncovered, for 1/2 hour at 325°.

Campfire Baked Beans—
American Indian style

SERVES FOUR

Serve with corn on the cob that has been left in its husks, thoroughly moistened, and steamed under hot ashes.

6 cups canned Great Northern beans	1/2 tsp dry mustard
	1/4 tsp ground cloves
Hot water to barely cover	3 tbsp minced onion
1 cup dark brown sugar	1/3 cup oil or margarine

Dig a hole in the ground large enough to hold 5–6 large stones and the beanpot.

Heat the stones in a campfire and place in the hole.

Mix all ingredients in a beanpot or casserole, adding salt to taste; cover tightly.

Place the pot on the stones and cover with hot ashes and sod.

Remove after 2–3 hours.

Crown of Beans Mexicali

Corona de Frijol

SERVES TWO TO THREE

Serve with fresh asparagus, crisp tacos, and a salad of fresh
tomatoes, cucumber, and green peppers, finely chopped, and
mixed with vinegar and oil to taste.

1 cup small red beans
3 cups water or Basic Broth
  (pp. 11–12)
1/2 cup chopped onion
3 tbsp oil
3/4 cup cheddar cheese,
  shredded

2 eggs, well beaten
1 tsp salt
1/8 to 1/4 tsp ground dried
  chili peppers
1/4 cup bread crumbs

Rinse and soak beans (pp. 5–6). Drain.

Pressure cook with water or broth and 1 tbsp oil (pp. 6–10).

Sauté the onions in 2 tbsp oil. Add beans and fry for five
minutes.

Grind beans, cheese, and onions together.

Add eggs, salt, peppers, and mix well.

Grease a casserole and sprinkle it with bread crumbs.

Pour in the bean mix and press down well.

Cover with bread crumbs; dot with butter or margarine.

Bake in a 350° oven about 25 minutes, uncovered.

East Indian Kedgeree

SERVES THREE TO FOUR

Serve with stewed tomatoes and eggplant (or okra) and Banana Sambol.

3 tbsp oil or butter
1/2 cup finely chopped onion
1 minced garlic clove
1 cup lentils
6 cups water or Basic Broth
   (pp. 11–12)

2 bay leaves
1/2 tsp cinnamon
12 ground cardamom seeds
1/4 tsp mace
6 whole cloves
1 cup raw rice

Sauté the onion and garlic in the oil.

Rinse lentils.

Combine all ingredients and pressure cook (pp. 6–10).

Place in a casserole, cover, and put in the oven at low heat until ready to serve.

Banana Sambol

SERVES THREE TO FOUR

4–5 green bananas
1/4 tsp ground red chili
   peppers
1 tbsp butter or oil
1 chopped large onion
1 minced garlic clove

2 green chili peppers, canned
   or fresh
1/2 tsp ground ginger
1/2 tsp ground cumin
1 tsp ground turmeric

Cut the bananas into 1/3-inch slices; sprinkle with the ground red chilis.

Fry the remaining ingredients over low heat.

Combine the bananas and spice mixture and allow to stand in the refrigerator for one day.

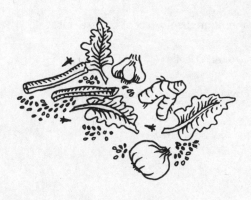

Escalloped Spinach

SERVES THREE TO FOUR

Serve with baked potatoes, stewed tomatoes, and carrot and celery sticks.

2 cans spinach, drained	1 1/2 tbsp white or wine
1 cup finely chopped onion	vinegar
1/3 cup sliced fresh	1/4 tsp salt
mushrooms	1/4 tsp freshly ground pepper
3 tbsp olive oil	2–3 drops Tabasco sauce
2 tbsp flour	1/8 tsp nutmeg
2 cups mashed tofu	Grated cheddar cheese
	(optional)

Sauté onion in olive oil until it is transparent.

Add flour and stir until browned.

Add all other ingredients except cheese; mix well.

Top with grated cheese.

Bake in covered skillet or casserole at 350° for 30 minutes.

Hearthside Baked Beans

SERVES THREE

Serve with brown bread and a coleslaw, using finely sliced cabbage and minced green peppers and onion with a dressing made of 2 parts oil to one part vinegar plus prepared mustard and sugar to taste.

1 cup soybeans	2 cups cooked rice
3 cups water	1/3 cup brown sugar
1 stalk celery	1/4 cup molasses
2 carrots	2 tbsp soy sauce
1 onion	2 tbsp cooking sherry or rum
5 tbsp oil	(optional)

Rinse and soak beans (pp. 5–6). Drain.

Combine with the vegetables cut in large pieces, oil, and water.

Pressure cook (pp. 6–10).

Turn off heat; reduce pressure gradually by allowing cooker to stand for 4–5 minutes.

Remove vegetables.

Combine beans with rice, brown sugar, molasses, soy sauce, and sherry; add salt to taste.

Bake, covered, at 300° for 2 hours, taking the cover off for the last 30 minutes or so for browning.

Lima Bean and Tomato Casserole

SERVES THREE TO FOUR

Serve with French-fried okra, green bean and sprout salad
(p. 43), and corn bread.

2 cups dried lima beans	1/2 cup chopped green
6 cups water or Basic Broth	pepper
(pp. 11–12)	1/4 tsp cayenne
1/2 cup olive oil	2 cups canned tomatoes (or
4 scallions, tops and bulbs	fresh)
chopped	Parmesan or shredded
	cheddar cheese

Rinse and soak limas (pp. 5–6). Drain.

Pressure cook with the water or broth and 1 tbsp oil for 5
minutes at 15-lb pressure or 10 minutes at 10-lb pressure
(pp. 6–10).

Reduce pressure gradually.

Sauté scallions in oil until yellow. Add green peppers and beans
and toss together for a few minutes. Add sugar and cayenne,
salt to taste.

Place in a greased casserole and cover with tomatoes.

Sprinkle with cheese.

Bake uncovered in a 350° oven for 30 minutes or more.

Lima Beans Fermière Française

SERVES THREE TO FOUR

Serve with green olive, bean sprout, and cabbage salad, and fried apple rings.

2 cups large dried lima beans	3 tbsp olive oil
6 cups water or Basic Broth (pp. 11–12)	1/4 tsp each pepper, savory, and nutmeg
1 tbsp oil	1/8 tsp fennel
1 cup chopped onion	1/4 cup finely chopped parsley
4 thinly sliced carrots	

Rinse and soak the beans (pp. 5–6). Drain.

Pressure cook (pp. 6–10) with the broth and oil for 5 minutes at 15-lb pressure or 10 minutes at 10-lb pressure.

Sauté the carrots and onions in the olive oil.

Combine all ingredients except parsley; add salt to taste.

Bake uncovered at 350° for 30 minutes or more.

Garnish liberally with the finely chopped parsley.

Minnehaha Baked Beans

SERVES THREE TO FOUR

Serve with baked yams and stewed tomatoes plus a light dessert
of diced tofu mixed with thawed frozen strawberries.

2 cups navy beans	1 tsp salt
2 qt water	1/2 cup brown sugar
1 tsp baking soda	1 small onion, minced
2 tbsp mild molasses	1/2 cup margarine or butter
1/2 tsp dry mustard	

Rinse beans. Cook for 30 minutes, covered, in 2 qt water to
which the baking soda has been added.

Turn off heat. Let stand for two hours, covered.

Drain.

Add remaining ingredients and water to barely cover the
mixture.

Cook in a tightly covered pot at minimal heat (no pressure) for
one hour or until tender. (This method keeps the bean skins
intact.)

Brown, uncovered, in the oven before serving.

New England Baked Beans

SERVES EIGHT

Serve with Boston brown bread and a spinach, bean sprout, and garlic salad.

4 cups navy beans	1/8 tsp ginger
4 qt water	2 tbsp sugar
2 tsp baking soda	1/4 cup molasses
3/4 tsp dry mustard	1 cup margarine
2 tsp salt	

Rinse beans. Cook for 30 minutes, in the 4 qt water to which 2 tsp baking soda has been added.

Turn off heat. Let stand for two hours, covered.

Drain.

Add 1 1/2 cups water (to barely cover beans) and the remaining ingredients.

Cook in a covered pot at minimal heat (no pressure) for one hour or until tender. (This method keeps the bean skins intact.)

Brown, uncovered, in the oven before serving.

Boston Brown Bread

MAKES FIVE CANS

1 cup corn meal
1 cup whole wheat flour
1/2 cup soy flour
1/2 cup white flour

1 tsp salt
3/4 cup molasses
2 cups buttermilk
1 cup raisins

Mix molasses and buttermilk.

Mix dry ingredients. Add raisins and wet ingredients.

Grease 5 16-oz cans.

Pour 1 cup batter into each can.

Cover tightly with foil.

Place on a trivet or rack in a large pot or pan.

Add boiling water to a depth of 2 inches.

Cover pot or pan and cook slowly 45 minutes to one hour until done (bread will be firm to the touch).

Store in freezer or refrigerator.

Piernik

SERVES THREE TO FOUR

Serve with baked squash and avocado/grapefruit salad.

1 cup dried soup peas
2 1/2 cups water or Basic
   Broth (pp. 11–12)
1 tsp salt
2 tbsp oil
1 cup sliced carrots

1/2 cup chopped onions
1/4 cup chopped celery
1 cup sliced mushrooms
2 tbsp soy sauce
1 cup sauerkraut

Rinse and soak the peas (pp. 5–6). Drain.

Pressure cook (pp. 6–10) with water or broth and 1 tbsp oil.

Reduce cooker pressure under cold water.

Fry carrots, onions, and mushrooms lightly together in 1 tbsp oil.

Add soy sauce; let set five minutes.

Oil a casserole; layer in peas, other vegetables, and sauerkraut. Cover. Bake 30 minutes at 350°

Plate National—Haiti

SERVES FOUR

Serve with bananas in rum (Bananes Au Rhum).

1 cup pinto beans	1 tbsp minced parsley
4 cups water or Basic Broth	1/2 tsp pepper
(pp. 11–12)	1/8 tsp cayenne
1/2 cup margarine	1/4 tsp ground cloves
1 minced garlic clove	1 cup rice
1 cup chopped onion	

Soak beans (pp. 5–6). Drain.

Sauté garlic, onion, and parsley in margarine; add pepper and cloves.

Combine all ingredients and pressure cook (pp. 6–10) for 15 minutes.

Reduce pressure.

Pour bean and rice mixture into a well-oiled casserole, season with salt, and bake in a very slow oven (250°) for 30 minutes. Add hot water if the mixture becomes too dry.

Bananes Au Rhum

SERVES THREE TO FOUR

6 large ripe bananas   3 tbsp rum
1/2 cup olive oil   1/4 icing sugar
1/2 tsp vanilla

Peel bananas and cut across in thin slices.

Fry in hot oil.

When lightly browned remove and drain on paper towelling.

Add vanilla to rum and sprinkle over bananas.

Sieve icing sugar over the top and serve cold.

Puerto Rican Baked Beans with Rum

Serve with corn bread and a mixed green salad of Cos lettuce, scallions, spinach, thinly sliced cabbage, and an oil and vinegar dressing to which a little taco sauce has been added.

2 cups black beans
8 cups water
2 tsp baking soda
1/2 cup vegetable oil
1 1/2 tsp salt
1/2 cup brown sugar

1/4 cup molasses
2 tsp dry mustard
1/4 cup dark rum
1/4 tsp thyme
1 medium onion
2 garlic cloves

Rinse beans. Cook for 30 minutes, covered, in the water to which the baking soda has been added.

Turn off heat. Let stand for two hours, covered.

Drain.

Add remaining ingredients and enough water to barely cover beans.

Cook in a covered pot at minimal heat (no pressure) for one hour or until tender. (This method tenderizes the bean skins without breaking them.)

Brown, uncovered, in the oven, until desired degree of juiciness is attained.

Tamale Pie

SERVES THREE TO FOUR

Serve with guacamole (p. 46) and hard rolls.

2 tbsp olive oil	1/8 tsp cayenne pepper
1 cup chopped white onions	1 cup water
2 cups whole kernel corn	1 cup yellow cornmeal
1/2 chopped green pepper	1/2 cup mashed tofu
2 cups canned tomatoes	1/2 cup chopped ripe olives
1 tsp salt	1 cup chopped nuts

Cook onion in olive oil until tender.

Add corn, green pepper, tomatoes, seasoning, and water.

Bring to boiling and add cornmeal gradually, stirring constantly.
Cook 20 minutes.

Add tofu, olives, nuts, and pour into an oiled casserole.

Bake at 350° for 45 minutes.

Vegetable Medley

SERVES FOUR

Serve with hot corn bread and mushroom and bean sprout salad (p. 47).

2 cups cooked soybeans
1 cup zucchini, chopped
1 cup chopped eggplant
1/2 cup chopped green
    pepper
2 garlic cloves
1/2 cup mushrooms

4 cups tomatoes
1/2 tsp sweet basil leaves
2 tsp oregano leaves
1/2 tsp chopped dry red chilis
2 tbsp minute tapioca
Parmesan cheese

Combine all ingredients, salt and pepper to taste, and bake at 325° for one hour.

Cover generously with Parmesan cheese for the last 30 minutes.

7 FEASTS FOR SPECIAL OCCASIONS

AN AMERICAN HERBAL FEAST

SERVES FOUR TO SIX

I

Iced Tomato Soup

2 lb tomatoes, peeled and
    chopped *or* 4 cups canned
    tomatoes
1 chopped medium
    cucumber

2 minced garlic cloves
1 cup diced tofu
1/3 cup vegetable or olive oil
1 tbsp lemon juice
1 tsp powdered cumin

Blend all ingredients, salt to taste. Serve as a soup with one
chunk of ice in each bowl.

II

Savoury Rice

2 cups natural rice
3 to 3 1/4 cups water
2 cups finely sliced white
    onions
1 cup sliced fresh
    mushrooms

2 cups frozen peas
2 tsp basil leaves
2 tbsp margarine or butter
Slivered toasted almonds
    (optional)

Combine rice and water in pressure cooker; cook 18 minutes
(pp. 6–10).

Reduce pressure gradually.

In the meantime, fry the onions at moderate heat until transparent.

Add mushrooms and peas; continue to fry at low heat.

Add rice, basil, and salt, freshly ground pepper, and Tabasco sauce to taste.

Serve in a casserole topped with the slivered almonds.

Carrots with Thyme
Scrub and trim twenty young fresh carrots.

Use whole, or cut diagonally; steam above lightly salted water, or cook until crisply tender in a small amount of unsalted water.

Melt 3 tbsp butter in a saucepan.

Add powdered or leaf thyme to taste.

Corn with Marjoram
3 cans creamed corn   3 tbsp margarine or butter
1/2 cup chopped onion   1/4 tsp marjoram
1/4 cup chopped green   Black pepper
  pepper

Sauté onions and green pepper in butter until transparent.

Add corn and marjoram; heat through.

Tarragon Salad Dressing

2 finely chopped scallions
   (including the green ends)
1/4 tsp salt
1/4 tsp white or black pepper
1/2 tsp Accent (optional)

1/4 tsp sugar
1/2 tsp tarragon leaves
1/3 cup white vinegar
2/3 cup salad or olive oil

Combine and chill. Serve on a mixed green salad.

III

Mint Cup

1 cup fresh or canned
   pineapple
1 cup fresh or canned
   grapefruit sections

1 cup fresh or mandarin
   oranges
1/4 cup strong cold spearmint
   or peppermint tea

Sweeten to taste and serve in small glasses.

Cold or hot pennyroyal or rosemary tea could add one more herbal flavour to the feast.

AN EAST INDIAN-STYLE FEAST

SERVES FOUR TO SIX

Serve this meal with a side dish of yoghurt and canned apricots sprinkled with fresh grated ginger; an Indian chutney (or spiced peaches); and an Indian hot pickle if available, or onion sambol.

I

Squash Curry

2 pkg frozen squash   1 tsp Indian curry powder
1/2 cup water   Ground Brazil nuts
4 tbsp butter

Cook squash with the water in a covered pan at low heat.

Meanwhile, fry the curry powder in the butter until the butter ceases to foam.

Combine squash and curry mixture. Salt to taste. Add a pinch of cayenne if a hotter taste is desired.

Serve over hot boiled rice and top with ground nuts.

Boiled Rice

3 cups white rice   Dash salt
3 1/2 cups water   2 tsp oil

Wash rice well.

Place in a large heavy-bottomed pan and add water, salt, and oil.

Place over high heat until rice begins to boil; then lower heat way down.

Do not stir. Remove cover after 18 minutes and check for tenderness. Rice should be firm but tender, and each kernel separate.

Split Pea Dhal

3 cups yellow (or green) split peas	1/3 cup margarine or butter
5 cups water	2 tsp crushed cumin seed, or 1 tsp powdered cumin
1 tsp salt	1/4 tsp cayenne pepper
1 tbsp oil	1/2 tsp black pepper
2 cups finely chopped onions	1 tsp powdered turmeric
1 tbsp black (or yellow) mustard seeds	Chopped parsley, chives, or mint

Combine peas, salt, oil, and water, and pressure cook (pp. 6–10).

Meanwhile, fry the mustard seeds in the butter until they begin to crackle; add the onion and fry till golden.

Add the cumin, cayenne, black pepper, and turmeric and fry until butter is absorbed.

Reduce pressure on peas. If they are too watery, boil down on low heat: the consistency should be soft and moist. To make the texture perfectly smooth, beat or blend.

Top each serving of the pea mixture with a spoonful of the fried spices; garnish with the chopped green herbs.

Onion Sambol

1 large onion	Juice of 1/2 lemon
1 medium cucumber	1/2 tsp salt
1 medium green pepper	1/2 tsp ground red chili peppers

Slice vegetables fine.

Combine with remaining ingredients.

Marinate for several hours or over night.

II

Indian Banana Dessert

12 ripe bananas, mashed	1/2 cup sugar
3/4 cup farina (Cream of Wheat)	1 1/2 tbsp butter
	1/4 tsp cinnamon

Mix all ingredients and cook very gently in a double boiler for three hours.

Pour out into a cake pan. Chill.

Cut into pieces before serving. Garnish with ground nuts and paprika.

A GREEK-STYLE FEAST

SERVES SIX

I

Vegetable salad

Salata

1/2 head cabbage shredded
1 cup cooked green beans
4 cups sliced cooked beets
1 tbsp capers

1 doz sliced black Greek olives
6 tbsp olive oil
4 tbsp vinegar
1 tsp mustard

Mix vegetables.

Mix oil, vinegar, and mustard and pour over vegetables.

Serve immediately.

Vine Leaves with Rice Filling

Nistisimes Dolmades

Serve hot or cold.

1 can vine leaves
1 cup rice
2/3 cup olive oil
1/3 cup lemon juice

4 cups water
3 cups finely chopped onions
2 tbsp tomato paste
2 tbsp chopped parsley or
    mint leaves

Put rice to soak in 2 cups hot water, until ready to use.

Sauté onions with the olive oil until transparent.

Drain rice. Add to onions. Continue sautéing at low heat.

Add tomato paste, chopped parsley or mint, and half of the lemon juice; heat.

Spread out the vine leaves one by one and place 1 tsp of the onion and rice mixture on each one. Starting from the stem of the vine leaf, turn in ends and roll tightly.

Arrange in layers in compact saucepan.

Add remaining lemon juice to 1 cup water; pour over the rolls.

Cover and bring to a boil for 5 minutes over high flame.

Reduce heat and cook 15 minutes.

Add 1 more cup of water; reduce heat to low and continue cooking until rice is tender.

Lentils with Egg Noodles

Kouloorea

2 cups lentils
3 1/2 cups water
1 tsp salt
1/2 cup olive oil
1 large onion, sliced fine
2 cups egg noodles (dry)

3 qt boiling water
2 cups tomato pulp (raw or
    cooked)
1/2 cup tomato sauce
2 tbsp parsley or mint leaves,
    minced

Rinse lentils and cook under pressure with the salt, 3 1/2 cups water, and 2 tbsp of the olive oil (pp. 6–10).

Meanwhile, cook the noodles in the boiling water for 3 minutes, or until tender but still firm. Drain.

Fry onions in the remainder of the olive oil over moderate heat, stirring frequently, until black, but not charred.

Layer lentils with onions, tomatoes, and noodles in a flat dish, or round casserole.

Top with tomato sauce and bake uncovered at 325° for 20 minutes.

Garnish with the minced parsley or mint before serving.

II

Spice Bars

Finikia

Serve cold.

1/4 cup sugar
1/4 cup orange juice
1 cup vegetable oil
1 tsp cinnamon

1/8 tsp nutmeg
3 1/2 cups flour
1 cup chopped pecans or
   walnuts

Blend oil, sugar, and seasonings.

Add orange juice and flour until a smooth dough is formed.

Knead gently; add nuts.

Form into 3-inch rolls.

Place on a greased baking sheet.

Bake at 325° for 35 minutes.

When well browned remove from oven.

While still warm dip quickly into a warm syrup made of 1 cup honey and 1/2 cup water.

AN ISRAELI-STYLE FEAST

SERVES SIX

I

Cloud Dumpling Soup

Luft-knaidlach

2 tbsp ground almonds (optional)	1 tsp salt
1/2 cup sliced onions	1/2 cup tofu
1 tbsp chopped parsley	1 egg
1/2 tsp grated lemon rind	6 tbsp olive oil
1/4-inch slice of fresh ginger (or nutmeg to taste)	3/4 cup Matzo meal
	1/4 tsp baking powder

Combine all ingredients except Matzo meal and baking powder and mix in an electric blender until smooth.

Combine with the Matzo meal and baking powder, which have been combined, mixing well.

Refrigerate half a day or overnight.

Form into small balls and cook, *covered*, for 30 minutes or more in Basic Broth (pp. 11-12) or chicken-flavoured bouillon.

II

Israeli Casserole

Mezid Adashim

3 cups lentils	1/2 cup chopped celery
6 cups water or Basic Broth (pp. 11–12)	2 tbsp minced parsley
	4 tbsp olive oil
2 cups finely chopped onion	4 tbsp flour
3 garlic cloves	1/4 tsp black pepper
	Tomato purée

Sauté the onion, celery, and garlic in 2 tbsp olive oil.

Rinse lentils.

Pressure cook (pp. 6–10) lentils with vegetables and water or broth for 10 minutes at 10-lb pressure or 5 minutes at 15-lb pressure.

Reduce pressure by placing cooker under cold water.

In a saucepan combine the rest of the oil and the flour; stir at moderate heat until brown.

Add the flour mixture and the pepper to the lentil mixture; salt to taste.

Pour into a casserole; top with the tomato purée.

Bake at 350° for 30 minutes.

Potato Pancakes

Latkes

4 large potatoes, well
  scrubbed and cut in eighths
1 onion
1/3 cup tofu
1 tsp salt

1/4 tsp freshly ground black
  pepper
3 tbsp potato starch or flour
1/2 tsp baking powder
1/2 cup oil

Combine all ingredients except oil in electric blender; mix until
smooth.

Heat the oil in a skillet; drop in the potato mixture by the
tablespoonful.

When brown on both sides, drain well, and put into a warm oven
until ready to serve.

These pancakes can be topped with raw or cooked applesauce
flavoured with nutmeg.

III

Fruit Kissel

Serve cold.

2 cups strawberries, fresh or
  frozen
2 cups rhubarb, fresh or
  frozen

1 3/4 cups water
4 tbsp cornstarch mixed with
  1/4 cup water
Honey or sugar to taste

Combine fruit and water and boil until fruit is soft.

Put through a food mill to make a purée.

Add sugar to taste.

Add the cornstarch mixture and cook over low heat for another five minutes.

A JAPANESE-STYLE FEAST

SERVES FOUR TO SIX

I

Miso Shiru Soup

Potatoes, onions, or greens can be added to this soup.

6 cups Basic Broth
   (pp. 11–12) or
   "Dashi-no-Moto"—
   a seaweed stock in dried
   form—(available at
   health food shops)

1 small can mushrooms
1/4 cup miso
1 cup diced tofu
2 tsp sherry (optional)
Twists of lemon or orange
   peel and sliced scallions

Bring broth and miso to a boil.

Reduce heat. Add tofu and sherry; heat through.

Garnish each serving with a twist of lemon or orange peel and
the scallions.

II

Soy Cucumber Salad

Sunomono

3 cups shredded or thinly
   sliced cucumber
1 tbsp salt
1 tbsp peanut or corn oil
1 tsp sesame oil (optional)

1/2 tsp sugar
1 tbsp Kikkoman soy sauce
   (Japanese)
1/2 tsp vinegar
1 tsp Accent

Sprinkle the cucumber with the salt. Put in a crock or pan and let it stand for eight hours or more, preferably with a plate on top of it, weighted down with a brick or a pan of water.

Rinse the cucumber thoroughly. Squeeze out all the water.

Mix with the other ingredients. Chill.

Serve in small bowls with or without lettuce. Garnish each serving with a light shake of cayenne pepper or paprika.

Vegetable Sukiyaki—traditionally made with beef

3 tbsp oil
1/2 cup Kikkoman soy sauce (Japanese)
2 tbsp sugar
1/4 cup white wine or sake
1 cup water
4 tsp dried Onion Soup Mix
3 onions, cut in 1/4-inch slices
16 scallions, cut in 1 1/2-inch lengths
1/2 lb fresh mushrooms or 1 large can mushrooms
4 stalks celery or 2 ribs celery cabbage cut in 1/4-inch slices
1 lb fresh spinach
2 medium zucchini cut in thin strips
1 cup bean sprouts
4 oz thin spaghetti or Japanese noodles
2 cups tofu, cubed

Mix soup mix with liquids to create a broth, and pour half the amount into a skillet or electric frying pan.

Slice the vegetables as attractively as possible and arrange half and half on two large plates.

Cook the spaghetti until barely tender in boiling, unsalted water; drain.

Cook half the vegetables at a time in the broth, keeping each kind separate; serve while they are still crisp.

Add half of the tofu and the spaghetti toward the end of the vegetable cooking period.

Serve from the pan at the table with hot boiled rice. If the meal is served with bowls and chopsticks the guests can hold their bowls of rice close to the pan as they lift out morsels of the cooked food with their chopsticks. Or the vegetables can be ladled out in separate bowls.

III

For dessert serve Japanese green tea and a slice of candied ginger or of Yokan, a candied red bean cake, available at Oriental specialty shops.

A LEBANESE-STYLE FEAST

SERVES FOUR

Lebanese Lentils

2 cups lentils
5 cups water or Basic Broth
  (pp. 11–12)

1 large sliced onion
4 tbsp olive oil

Pressure cook washed lentils (pp. 6–10).

Meanwhile, fry the onion in the olive oil, stirring steadily until it is *black*, but not charred.

Reduce pressure in the cooker by dousing with cold water.

Simmer onions and lentils together until flavours are blended. Add salt to taste. When ready to serve, the mixture should be moist but not soupy.

Lebanese Red Rice

1/2 large chopped onion
2 minced garlic cloves
2 tbsp olive oil
2 cups white rice

1 cup tomato purée
2 cups boiling water or Basic
  Broth (pp. 11–12)

Fry onion and garlic in oil until transparent.

Add the rice and fry until lightly toasted.

Add purée and boiling broth or water.

Cover and simmer over low heat until all liquid has been absorbed, about 15 minutes. Do not stir.

Eggplant Lebanese

1 medium eggplant
  (unpeeled)
olive oil
1/4 cup cornmeal or bread
  crumbs

1/4 tsp salt
1/2 cup tahini (sesame butter)
1/4 cup fresh lemon juice
1/3 cup water
Chopped scallions

Slice the eggplant into 1/2-inch slices; cut each slice into 4 equal parts.

Mix the cornmeal or bread crumbs and salt.

Dip the eggplant slices in the olive oil and then the cornmeal mixture.

Grill in a flat pan until crisp and brown (about 3 minutes on each side).

Serve hot with a thin sauce made of the tahini, lemon juice, water, finely chopped scallions, and salt to taste.

Salad Tabouli

Serve on fresh lettuce or grape leaves.

1 cup bulgur (parboiled
  cracked wheat)
4 bunches fresh parsley
4 tomatoes
1 tsp dried mint leaves *or* 1
  bunch fresh mint leaves

1 bunch scallions
1/4 cup olive oil
1/4 cup lemon juice
1 tsp cinnamon

Soak the bulgur in water for half an hour.

Wash and mince the parsley and mint leaves fine.

Chop the tomatoes and scallions coarsely.

Squeeze out excess water from the bulgur.

Mix it with the chopped mint, parsley, tomatoes, and scallions.

Add the cinnamon, lemon juice, and olive oil mixed with salt and freshly ground pepper to taste. Chill.

Middle Eastern bread (pitta) could be another authentic addition to the meal.

A truly elegant dessert would be Turkish coffee and baklava (available at Greek or Lebanese specialty shops). Or cold stewed pears with a slice of halva.

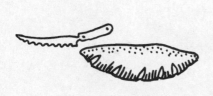

A MEXICAN-STYLE FEAST

SERVES FOUR

I

Serve these entrées with corn on the cob or kernel corn flavoured with red or green chili peppers.

Mexican Rice

Arroz Mexicano

3 cups white rice
4 tbsp margarine or butter
2 tbsp olive oil
1 tsp cumin seed
1 tsp salt
1/2 chopped green pepper

2 minced garlic cloves
1 1/2 cups chopped onion
2 large tomatoes, chopped *or*
    2 cups canned tomatoes
4 cups hot Basic Broth
    (pp. 11–12) or tomato juice

Fry the rice in the oil until it begins to brown.

Add the rest of the ingredients, cover, and cook over low heat until the stock has been absorbed and the rice is soft.

Beans with Sauce

Frijoles con Mole

2 cups pink or kidney beans
6 cups water or Basic Broth
  (pp. 11–12)
2 cups canned tomatoes
3 tbsp catsup
1 cup chopped onion
1 minced garlic clove
1/2 cup chopped green
  pepper

1/2 tsp crushed rosemary
  leaves
2 tsp chili powder
1 tbsp grated bitter chocolate
1 tsp Accent (optional)
1/4 to 1/2 tsp dried ground chili
  peppers
Salt to taste
Tabasco

Wash and soak the beans (pp. 5–6). Drain.

Add remaining ingredients and pressure cook (pp. 6–10).

Reduce pressure gradually.

Add salt and Tabasco to taste; serve garnished with fresh
chopped parsley or scallions.

Apple Pineapple Salad

Ensalada de Piña y Manzana

4 tart apples
1 cup chopped pineapple
  (fresh, if possible)
1/4 tsp salt

2 tbsp lemon juice
4 tbsp sugar
1/4 cup sherry

Peel and core apples; chop or dice.

Combine all ingredients and chill.

II

Raisin Tortillas

Capirotada

1 cup raisins   1/4 cup sugar
1 1/2 cups water   4–5 flour tortillas
2 cinnamon sticks   grated lemon rind

Cook the raisins with the cinnamon, sugar, and water, for 20 minutes at low heat, or until raisins are plump.

Layer the raisins and the tortillas in a round casserole or frying pan. Pour the raisin juice over the top layer, and sprinkle with lemon rind.

Cool. Cut into 2-inch squares and serve as an after-dinner sweet.

Glossary

"I was determined to know beans." Henry David Thoreau

Accent monosodium glutimate—meat tenderizer.

Alfalfa the seeds are used for making bean sprouts.

Black beans (or turtle soup beans) used in Mexico as a dietary staple.

Black-eyed peas (cow peas, black-eyed beans) a Southern favourite served with greens.

Brown beans a favourite among Swedish people for making sweet/sour beans.

Chickpeas (garbanzos) traditionally used in East Indian, Middle Eastern, and Latin American cultures. Sproutable.

Cornstarch cornflour.

Fava beans (broad beans) a brown bean resembling a large lima bean, but stronger in taste.

Great Northern beans a white bean used for soups and baked beans in the United States.

Green beans french beans.

Kidney beans a large red bean used for hearty dishes such as chili and soups.

Lentils sproutable, and a standby for soups and hot dishes.

Lima beans (butter beans) small and large forms, available dry and canned.

Miso fermented soybean paste.

Mung beans tiny sproutable beans which can also be used for cooking.

Navy beans (pea beans) popular in the United States for soup.

Peanuts available in raw and roasted forms; raw beans are a common ingredient in South Asian cooking.

Pink beans very smooth in texture and mild in taste.

135

Pinto beans   a mottled red bean of soft texture and smoothness when cooked.

Potato starch   potato flour.

Red beans (azuki beans)   particularly good in combination with rice or in sweet bean paste used in Oriental cooking.

Scallions   spring onions.

Skillet   shallow casserole or frying pan.

Soup peas   whole dried green peas.

Soybeans   the highest in available protein of all legumes. Sproutable. Available as: whole dried, grits (partially cooked, defatted bits that give a nutty texture to cooked cereals, breads, biscuits, and casseroles), soy milk, soy flour, toasted and salted, bean curd (tofu), or miso.

Split peas   both yellow and green; used as a staple food (called *dhal*) in India; combines well with curry powder.

Taco   a hot tortilla, rolled up around fillings like beans or crushed green chilis; often served with added fresh onion or tomato.

Tamari   concentrated sauce similar to soy sauce, but with a distinctive, slightly strong flavour.

Wax beans   broad beans, available fresh, frozen and canned.

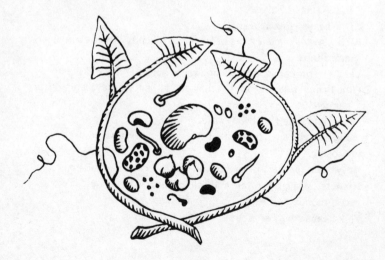

INDEX